G000255766

EXPLORING
THE ITCHEN WA.

Also in this series

Exploring the Ridgeway

Exploring the Pilgrims' Way

Exploring the Thames Valley
Kingston to Goring

Exploring the Thames Valley
Wallingford, Oxford & The Upper Thames

Other Walking Guides available from Countryside Books:

Avon Rambles
Bedfordshire Rambles
Buckinghamshire Rambles
Cambridgeshire Rambles
Dorset Rambles
Essex Rambles
Gloucestershire Rambles
Hertfordshire Rambles
Kent Rambles

Middlesex Rambles
Oxfordshire Rambles
Somerset Rambles
Suffolk Rambles
Surrey Rambles
East Sussex Rambles
West Sussex Rambles
Wiltshire Rambles

Walks in the Chilterns
Walks around the Downs
New Forest Walks
Short Walks in the New Forest
The Test Way
The Wayfarers Walk
New Forest Companion
In the Steps of Jane Austen
In the Steps of Thomas Hardy

EXPLORING THE ITCHEN WAY

Richard Kenchington

COUNTRYSIDE BOOKS
NEWBURY, BERKSHIRE

First Published 1990
© Richard Kenchington 1990

All rights reserved
No reproduction permitted
without the prior permission
of the publishers:

COUNTRYSIDE BOOKS
3, Catherine Road
Newbury, Berkshire

ISBN 1 85306 083 6

Cover photograph of the Itchen near Shawford
taken by Tony Knight
Sketch maps by the author

Produced through MRM Associates Ltd., Reading
Typeset by Acorn Bookwork, Salisbury
Printed in England by JW Arrowsmith Ltd., Bristol

Contents

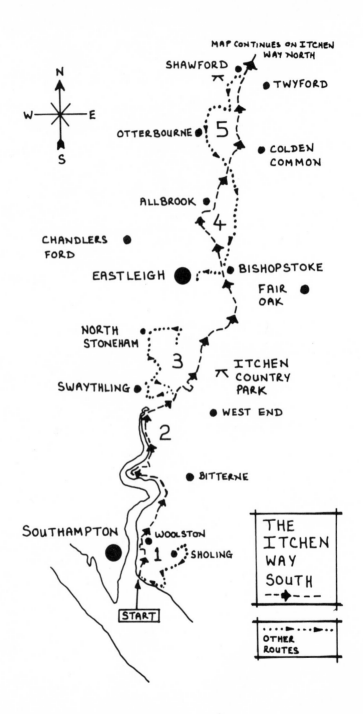

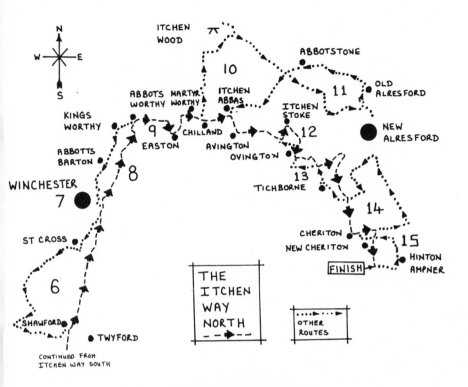

KEY TO THE ITCHEN WAY

Introduction

The river Itchen flows through some of the most beautiful countryside in Hampshire, from its source near the rural village of Hinton Ampner down to the port of Southampton. Starting life where several springs combine to form a dappled brook, the Itchen flows past old mills and water meadows near to the fascinating old town of Alresford with its nearby watercress beds. The river then meanders amongst meadows and marshes, past delightful Hampshire villages, to flow through the historic city of Winchester. The Itchen then heads south to eventually reach the parklands and urban fringes of Eastleigh and Southampton where it joins its sister river, the Test, to flow into Southampton Water.

The potential for developing the Itchen for river traffic was seen back in the 12th century when Godfrey de Lucy attempted to make the river navigable from Southampton as far as Alresford. Further attempts were made at the end of the 17th century, resulting in the opening in 1710 of the Navigation, connecting Winchester to the south coast sea trading routes at Southampton Water. A navigation is a waterway which makes use of sections of river and not solely an artificial cut, which would make it a canal. In this case it was also used to distribute water to a system of water meadows which were flooded in the early spring to encourage and enhance the growth of grass for the feeding of farm animals.

As a trade route the navigation was not a successful venture and the arrival of the railways brought the end in 1869 when the last barge carrying coal made its way up to Winchester. Today, the navigation provides a wealth of interest along its route for the industrial archaeologist and those looking for further information would do well to read *The Itchen Navigation* by Edwin Course.

My original idea to write a small pamphlet on a walk along the towpath of the navigation on rights of way from Southampton to Winchester gradually developed into this book of 15 walks exploring the countryside around the Itchen all the way to its source and to call the complete route the Itchen Way.

The concept of the Itchen Way is to form a two day walk up the river, stopping overnight at Winchester (perhaps at the Youth Hostel) and linking at the upper end of the river Itchen with the Wayfarers Walk and at the southern end with the Solent Way. The whole of the Itchen Way is incorporated into this book and if you are doing the full 27 mile walk the relevant sections are clearly indicated in each chapter. For those who prefer to sample the delights of the Itchen Valley in smaller doses, I have arranged the book as a series of individual walks, most of them circular, taking in sections of the Itchen Way and its surrounding glorious countryside. These rambles will give you an enjoyable sense of exploring the river from mouth to source, each providing a morning or afternoon's enjoyment in the open air.

I have supplied detailed maps of the route of each walk but should you feel the need for an Ordnance Survey map, the whole walk is covered by Sheet 185 in the 1:50 000 series, except for Southampton, which is covered by Sheet 196.

Each walk includes a section of historical notes to points of interest along the route.

If you can suggest any way in which future editions of this book can be updated, improved or corrected I should be pleased to hear from you. Finally if you have enjoyed these walks and want to continue your exploration of the area I would thoroughly recommend joining one of the Groups of the Ramblers' Association which are based at Southampton, East-leigh or Winchester. The addresses of the current officers of the Groups can be obtained at any local library. There are over 500 walks a year organised by these three Groups in Hampshire, Dorset, Wiltshire, Berkshire, Surrey and Sussex plus numerous social events.

The preparation of this book has given me much enjoyment. I trust that you will gain as much pleasure in using it.

Richard Kenchington
March 1990

9

Sholing to Bitterne

Introduction: Deep in the urban area of Southampton at Sholing Station, the first walk makes use of the city's green spaces
by visiting Millers Pond and then through the mature trees of
Mayfield Park with its muddy marshland to emerge on Weston
Shore with its panoramic views of Southampton Water and the
docks and down river to Calshot. Then it is up the estuary of
the river Itchen under the striking Itchen Toll Bridge and, near
Spitfire Quay it turns up to cross the parkland of Peartree
Green to its historic church. With good views of the marinas
and wharfs on the Itchen you follow a long curve in the river
above the birds on the mudflats opposite Millstone Point. At
Northam Bridge near Bitterne Manor House there is a glimpse
of what remains of the Roman town of Clausentum before
returning on the train from Bitterne to Sholing Station.

Distance: About 5 miles (7.8 km) of easy walking, strong shoes
required but boots would be necessary after heavy rain because
Mayfield Park can be muddy.

Return: By Rail from Bitterne Station to Sholing Station. An
hourly service 7 days a week. A journey of six minutes. The
train stops at Woolston en route.

Parking: No facilities at the station but street parking nearby.

Itchen Way – Weston Shore to Bitterne Station: This starts part
way through this walk on page 15 where the walk connects at
Weston Jetty with the Solent Way. On reaching Bitterne
Station to continue the Itchen Way turn to the start of Walk
Two on page 21.

11

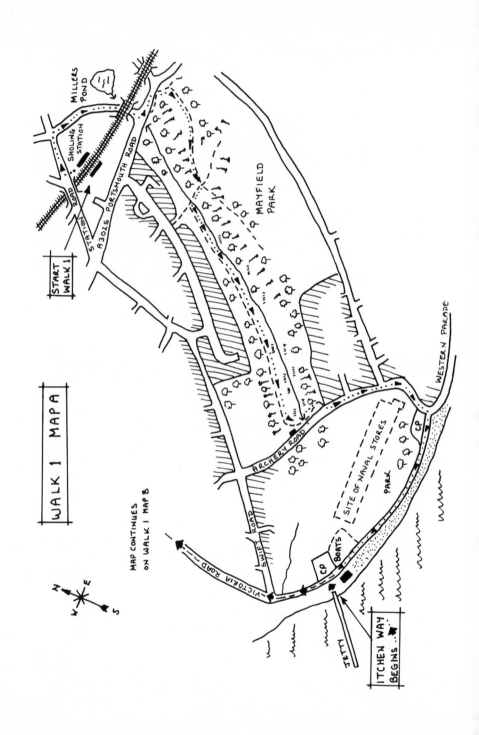

WALK 1 MAP A

START WALK 1

MILLERS POND

SHOLING STATION

STATION ROAD

A3025 PORTSMOUTH ROAD

MAYFIELD PARK

WESTERN PARADE

ARCHERY ROAD

SITE OF NAVAL STORES

PARK

CP

SWIFT ROAD

VICTORIA ROAD

CP

BOATS

CP

JETTY

ITCHEN WAY BEGINS...

MAP CONTINUES ON WALK 1 MAP B

N
W E
S

The Walk: Sholing Railway Station is an unmanned halt and there is only one exit and that from the eastbound platform up onto Station Road. When on the road turn right and head east for 100 metres to the junction with Spring Road and then turn right again to follow Spring Road downhill. After 200 metres there is the unkempt Millers Pond on the left. Pass under the three arched brick-built viaduct carrying the railway to reach the Portsmouth Road beyond.

Cross over the Portsmouth Road taking great care and turn left following a footway for 50 metres to reach a set of traffic lights. Bear right up a steep slope along a gravel path, forking right almost immediately, along and above a gulley containing a stream and a lot of rhododendrons. You are now in Mayfield Park with its attractive mature trees. Two hundred metres from the Portsmouth Road a specially constructed path with retaining sleepers drops diagonally down to the valley floor. The Mayfield Park playing fields and the grassy slopes on its northern slope appear on your left after 50 metres. Look here for a well defined track on your right which heads towards the stream and crosses it via a wooden footbridge.

Turn left after the bridge, following the north bank of the stream below the houses in Archery Grove. The track is muddy and roughly follows the line of a pipeline. A lot of wildlife survives in this much abused valley largely because the valley floor is so wet. Over 26 different types of tree have been recorded in this park. After keeping along the edge of these wetlands, in ½ mile you reach the point where Archery Road crosses the valley. The road is above and beyond a toilet block. At this point do not climb up to the road but turn left and go down to cross the valley where the waters collect to go through a culvert under the road. Climb up the other side and, on reaching the top, turn right for 25 metres to come out onto Archery Road next to a petrol filling station.

Turn left and follow Archery Road south-eastwards and after ½ mile you reach the shores of Southampton Water. To the right is the site of the former Royal Naval Stores Depot which has been sold for residential and industrial redevelopment so undoubtedly this area will be undergoing change in the

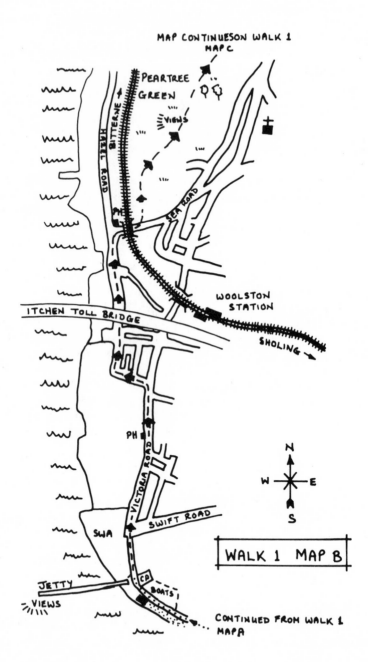

MAP CONTINUES ON WALK 1
MAP C

PEARTREE
GREEN

VIEWS

HAZEL ROAD

BITTERNE

SEA ROAD

PH

ITCHEN TOLL BRIDGE

WOOLSTON
STATION

SHOLING

PH

VICTORIA ROAD

SWIFT ROAD

N
W — E
S

WALK 1   MAP B

SWA

JETTY

VIEWS

CP

BOATS

CONTINUED FROM WALK 1
MAP A

near future. From Weston Shore you can look across to Hythe and downstream towards Fawley and Calshot Spit. On reaching the shoreline turn right and follow a footpath/ cycleway north-westwards towards Weston Point. At low tide there is plenty of birdlife on the mud flats.

After ½ mile you reach the Southampton Sailing Club, its boatyard and Weston Jetty which is **the start of the Itchen Way**. The jetty is currently open to the public by courtesy of the Southern Water Authority and from here there are views out to the confluence of the river Test and the river Itchen and downstream to the Isle of Wight. Upstream you can see the centre of Southampton and the new Ocean Village complex.

There is a car park at Weston Point. Leave it northwards along a road to the junction of Swift Road and Victoria Road. Proceed up Victoria Road passing on the left the Southern Water Authority sewer works. You will be able to sense that you are on the right route! The Vosper Thorneycroft yard occupies the river frontage to your left. Go past The Victoria public house at the entrance to the yard and a cafe on the other side of the road and then left down Keswick Road, turning left in 50 metres to continue along Keswick Road. Turn right at the bottom and along Wharf Road towards the new Itchen Toll Bridge. Just before the bridge on your left is the site of the slipway of the former Woolston floating bridge and ferry. (There is a pedestrian route up onto the new bridge if you wish to enjoy the good views up and downstream.)

Follow Hazel Road ahead, going under the new toll bridge past the memorial to Reginald Joseph Mitchell, the designer of the Spitfire aircraft. At the foreshore near the Southampton Rowing Club and The Yacht Tavern turn right into Sea Road and under the railway. Turn left immediately after passing under the bridge and up a bank onto Peartree Green a large piece of open grassland managed as a park by Southampton City Council. Once over the bank you drop down into a bowl and then head north-east on an undefined route, gradually uphill, with magnificent views back across the lower reaches of the Itchen. The aim is to get to the north-east corner of the parkland and the junction of Peartree Avenue and Osterley

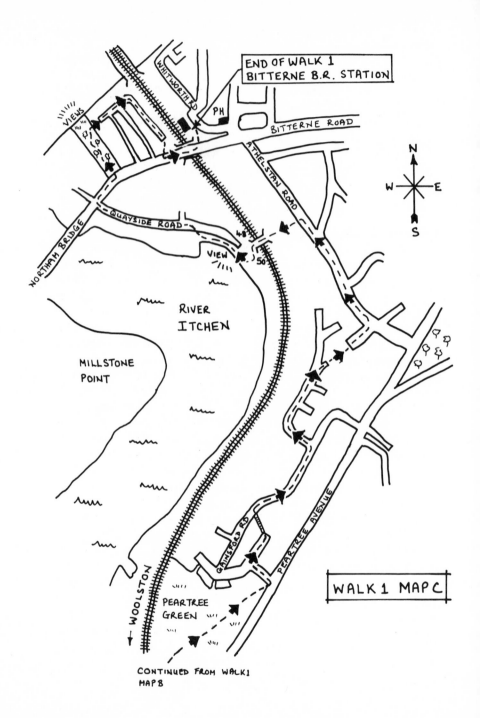

Road. Off to the right (east) is Pear Tree church, first dedicated in 1620.

Turn immediately left down Osterley Road and then right along that part of Bryanston Road which is a cul-de-sac. At the turning circle turn down left along a steep, stepped pathway to Gainsford Road below. Turn right to follow that road north-eastwards and then turn left down Braeside Road where there is a fine view across the river. Lower down, Braeside Road turns right, north-eastwards. Follow it to the point where Bronte Way bends down to the left. Here you continue straight on up a path linking to the end of Chine Avenue, a small cul-de-sac which takes you out onto Athelstan Road. Turn left and follow this main road north-west, circling around a large bend in the river Itchen below. Athelstan Road is followed until you get to a footpath/cycleway leaving the road on the left between Numbers 48 and 50. Follow the tarmac pathway over the railway line and down to the Itchen foreshore where there are good views downstream.

Turn right and follow a footpath along the riverbank adjacent to the housing at the eastern end of Quayside Road which the path joins in 300 metres. Continue along Quayside Road westwards until you meet the main Bitterne Road where you should cross over with care to the other side and turn right. Almost immediately on your left is the entrance to Bitterne Manor House and just beyond in the trees is a Southampton City park. Here are some of the barely traceable remains of Clausentum, the Roman town. Go through the park and at the other end you break out onto the bank of the river Itchen with a view upstream as far as the bridge carrying the St Denys to Bitterne railway. There is a short footpath connecting eastwards through to Vespasian Road. Take it and continue right to the eastern end of the road where there is a right turn into Chafen Road at the southern end of which there is a footpath link up to the Bitterne road. Turn left and go east over the railway bridge where there is a pedestrian walkway down to the east side of Bitterne Railway Station.

Historical Notes

Southampton: Ine, King of Wessex (AD 688–729) is thought to have created the right economically stable conditions for the establishment of the 40 hectare Saxon town of Hamwic or Hamtun in the area around the present day St Mary's church on the flat ground to the west of the Itchen. This town, laid out on a grid pattern, lasted until the mid 9th century, benefiting from being on the international trade routes along the west coast of Europe until it died out through Viking invasions. The town rapidly declined but another on the west side of the strip of land between the Itchen and the Test was established and flourishing by Norman times. In 1014 King Canute was proclaimed King in Southampton.

Trade with France provided great wealth for the town in the 12th century. Henry II (1133–1189) had a castle and a hall used as a store. Trade was badly affected by the loss of Normandy and Anjou by King John (1167–1216). (Number 58, French Street is a complete 13th century house.) The town was destroyed by French and Genoese who landed from galleys on the undefended West Quay in October 1338 at the beginning of the Hundred Years War which lasted until 1453. After this raid the main walls of the town were completed with seven gateways and 29 towers. Henry V passed through the Westgate on his way to victory at Agincourt in 1415. In the 15th century there was a large Italian community and such fine buildings as the Tudor House (a museum since 1912) date from that era. The 16th century Elizabethan period brought decay through a loss of international trade. The Pilgrim Fathers in the *Mayflower* and *Speedwell* set out from the town on 15th August 1620 on the way to the New World.

In the 18th century Londoners came to the town for sea bathing and the spa waters, and constructed a range of suburbs of substantial houses in picturesque parkland. The 19th century brought the first paddle steamers to cross to the Isle of Wight in 1820, the railways in 1838–40 and the first steamships to use Southampton Docks in 1842. Between 1841 and 1900 the population rose from 27,000 to 105,000.

The fateful voyage of the *Titanic* started here in April 1912 which brought the loss of many local people. The First World War saw 7 million men pass through the town and a massive ammunition industry was established. The Western Docks were built in the 1930s. The German Blitz of November and December 1940 destroyed much of the historical town centre but Southampton played a central role in the June 1944 Normandy landings when 2 million men passed through the town. The loss of the *Queen Mary*, *Queen Elizabeth* and the other famous liners and flying boats has not inhibited the continued growth of the town which is now set well to prosper in the 21st century.

Solent Way: This is the 60 mile long distance path met at Weston Shore. The route is from Milford on Sea along the Hampshire coastline to Emsworth. It is described in a book written by Barry Shurlock, published by Hampshire County Council Recreation Department.

Southampton Hall of Aviation: This museum is on the west side of the river Itchen and if you go over the Toll Bridge and bear left you will find it in Albert Road South. Here the story of RJ Mitchell, the Spitfire and the aviation history of the Southampton area is excellently set out with many famous historical aircraft exhibits.

Pear Tree Church: A book written in 1985 by DE Corps and available at the church is a detailed history of the area around Itchen Ferry and Woolston. The book also recalls a letter written by Jane Austen during her stay in Southampton between 1806 and 1809 when she recounted a traverse of the Itchen by ferry and a walk up Sea Road, across Peartree Green and onto Chessel House at Bitterne.

Clausentum: see Historical Notes in Walk Two.

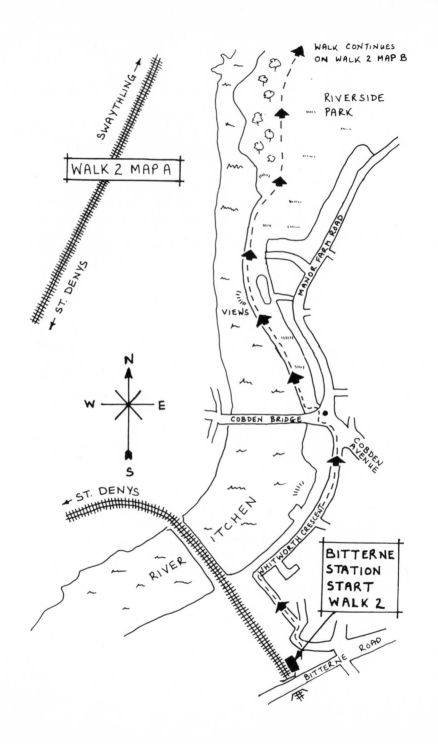

Bitterne to Swaythling

Introduction: From Bitterne Station this walk seeks out the east bank of the river Itchen where along Whitworth Crescent there are pretty little private wharfs. After the Clock Tower and Cobden Bridge the walk explores that part of the Itchen valley in the City of Southampton which has been protected from development. The route is through Riverside Park with its swans, model railway track and numerous sports pitches. Woodmill Lane marks the start of the Itchen Navigation which is followed through Townhill Park with its many ducks. On reaching the old hump-backed Mans Bridge the walk returns along the other side of the river along Monks Path, across Monks Brook to visit the Norman church at South Stoneham before reaching Swaythling Station and the train back to Bitterne.

Distance: 2½ miles (4.2 km) of very easy walking, only ordinary shoes required. Well surfaced paths throughout.

Return: By rail from Swaythling Station, changing at St Denys to return to Bitterne Station. An hourly service seven days a week. Journey time nine minutes including change of trains.

Parking: Parking at Bitterne Station for customers of British Rail. Street parking also available nearby.

Itchen Way – Bitterne Station to Mans Bridge: This second section of the Itchen Way starts with this walk at Bitterne Station but leaves it part way through the walk at Mans Bridge to continue on Walk Three at page 30.

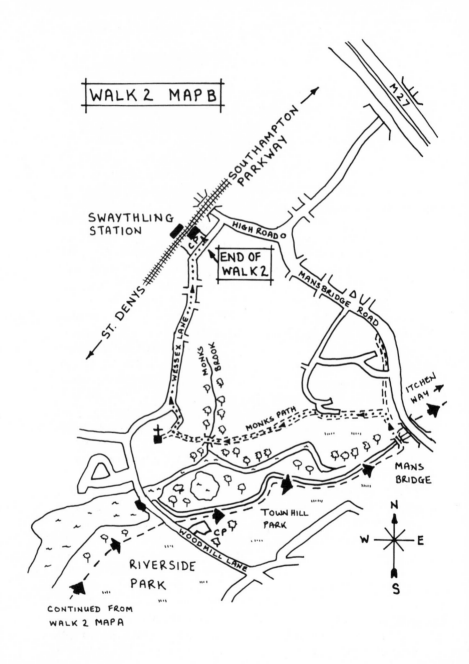

The Walk: Bitterne Station is on Macnaghten Road. Head north around a sharp bend and left into Whitworth Road and at the other end follow the road right into Whitworth Crescent which should be followed until you get to Cobden Bridge which is visible ahead. Along Whitworth Crescent there is a series of pleasure wharfs and some major new housing projects. At the bridge, cross over the pedestrian crossing to the clock tower and left past the toilets to join the riverside path through Cobden Meadows. The road walking is now at an end for a while.

The river is followed past a model locomotive track. There are houses on the right in River View Road and then you enter Riverside Park. There is a tarmac path all the way to Woodmill Lane Bridge, but there are opportunities to leave it on the left to explore routes closer to the river bank.

At Woodmill Lane cross over to follow the start of the Itchen Navigation along the east bank towards Mans Bridge. There is a wide, well made path all along the ½ mile to the old, stone, hump-backed bridge. Cross over it. Here those following the Itchen Way leave this walk. For the through route on **The Itchen Way** to Winchester, go immediately right and under the new Mans Bridge and continue at Walk Three, page 30.

This walk to Swaythling continues westward on the south side of the new road. When you reach a car park on the left, turn left to follow a tarmac path along the edge of the urban area to the north with the green fields of the valley floor to your left.

The path leads into a small cul-de-sac called Itchen View which in turn leads into Meadowside Close. Here immediately bear left to continue in the same direction along Monks Path. After passing further new development on the right, the path drops into a shallow gulley containing Monks Brook which is crossed by a footbridge. Once on the other side there is a very slight climb along a tarmac path between fences to emerge at the parish church of St Mary.

Bear right at the church to follow the entrance road out onto Wessex Lane in 100 metres. Cross over the road and turn right, following the undulating footway on the west side. There are halls of residence of Southampton University on both sides of the road. When some tennis courts are reached on the left it is necessary to cross over Wessex Lane to follow the footway on the east side around a double bend to reach Swaythling Railway Station.

Historical Notes

'Southampton Natural History Guide': This 163 page document, produced by the Southampton Schools Conservation Corps in 1987, contains a detailed analysis of the habitats, plant and wildlife of Millers Pond, Mayfield Park, Weston Shore, Peartree Green, Riverside Park and Mansbridge through which Walks One and Two pass.

Clausentum: The history of the area in the bend of the river west of Bitterne Station on which the Roman port, fort and town was constructed is set out in detail in a Ministry of Works Archaeological Report entitled *Excavations at Clausentum, Southampton 1951 – 54* by M Aylwin Cotton and PW Gathercole, published by HMSO in 1958.

Parish Church of St Mary, South Stoneham: Looking every bit like the traditional English country church, this building of Norman origin has witnessed the growth of the urban area of Southampton and the demise of the ancient parish of South Stoneham which embraced a wide area from Otterbourne in the north, Botley in the east and Southampton Common in the west. At the church there is a brief guide leaflet and the literature of the South Stoneham Trust which was formed to foster an interest in local history. This will give a greater appreciation of this picturesque spot.

'**The Southampton and Netley Railway**': The title of a book by Edwin Course, published by the City of Southampton in 1973. It relates the history of the line opened in 1866 from St Denys (formerly Portswood) to Netley and used in both Walks One and Two. A more recent book *South Coast Railways – Portsmouth to Southampton* by Vic Mitchell and Keith Smith, published in 1986 by Middleton Press, contains numerous plans and photographs of the stations visited. The same authors have produced a similar book on the line between Woking and Southampton used in later walks.

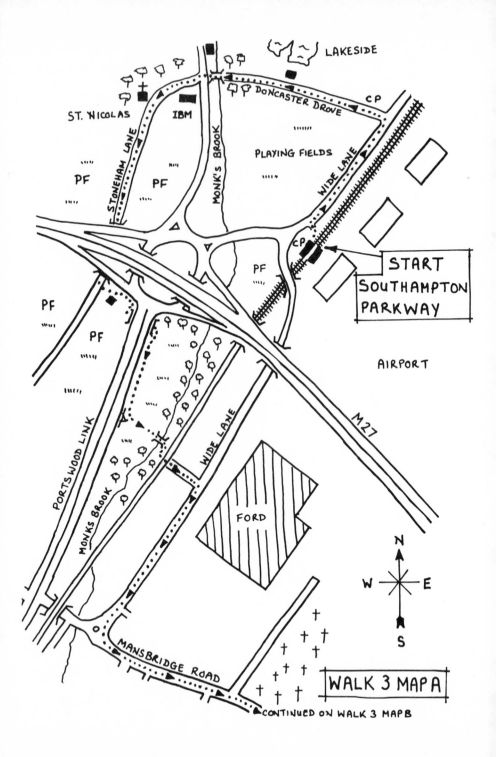

LAKESIDE

DONCASTER DROVE

CP

ST. NICOLAS

IBM

PLAYING FIELDS

PF

PF

Stoneham Lane

Monk's Brook

Wide Lane

CP

START

SOUTHAMPTON

PARKWAY

PF

PF

PF

AIRPORT

Portswood Link

Monks Brook

Wide Lane

FORD

M27

N

W ⊕ E

S

MANSBRIDGE ROAD

WALK 3 MAP A

CONTINUED ON WALK 3 MAP B

Southampton Parkway to Eastleigh

Introduction: This walk shows the precious urban fringe areas between Eastleigh and Southampton at their best and introduces the first section of open countryside along the Itchen Valley. From Southampton Parkway the walk goes between playing fields and the recently created Lakeside Park along Doncaster Drove and then along Stoneham Lane to visit St Nicolas church. After going under the M27 and the Portswood Link the hidden valley of Monks Brook is explored before setting off from Mans Bridge up the Itchen Navigation to Bishopstoke. With Eastleigh Airport to the west and the nature reserve of the Itchen Valley Country Park to the east, there is much plant and wildlife to see amongst the redundant locks and the disused water meadows. By the time the Barton river is crossed on a novel footbridge Bishopstoke and Stoke Park Woods come into view. A pub lunch at one of the good pubs at Bishopstoke and a visit to the museum of Eastleigh would complement this walk before returning by train from Eastleigh to Southampton Parkway.

Distance: Just over 6 miles (9.8 km) of easy walking but traffic particularly at peak periods poses a danger to walkers and for this reason it is not suitable for children. Strong shoes or walking boots recommended.

Return: By rail from Eastleigh station to Southampton Parkway is recommended as there is nothing attractive about the road walk between them. A service at least once an hour, seven days a week and a five minute journey time.

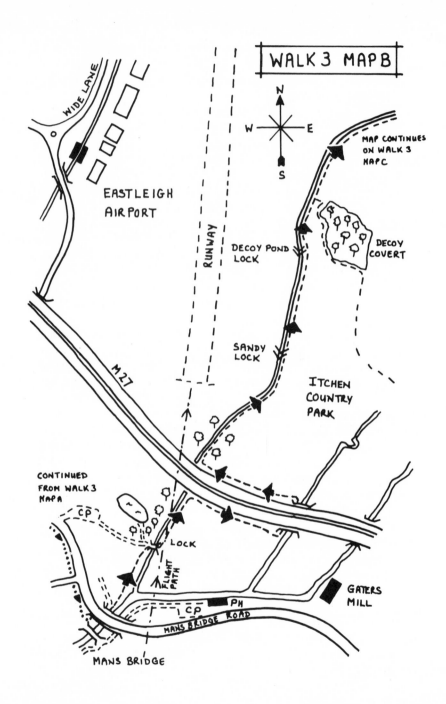

WALK 3 MAP B

WIDE LANE

EASTLEIGH AIRPORT

N
W E
S

MAP CONTINUES ON WALK 3 MAP C

RUNWAY

DECOY POND LOCK

DECOY COVERT

SANDY LOCK

M27

ITCHEN COUNTRY PARK

CONTINUED FROM WALK 3 MAP A

CP

LOCK

FLIGHT PATH

CP

PH

GATERS MILL

MANS BRIDGE ROAD

MANS BRIDGE

Parking: Available at Southampton Parkway for railway travellers. The car park is often nearly full during weekdays with commuters. There is a car park at Lakeside – see first paragraph of The Walk section.

Itchen Way – Mans Bridge to Bishopstoke: This third section of the Itchen Way starts part way through this walk at Mans Bridge on page 30 and continues up the Itchen Navigation until finishing at the B3037 at Bishopstoke where it is necessary to turn to the start of Walk Four on page 35.

The Walk: Southampton Parkway, originally Southampton Airport station, opened in 1966 to serve the adjacent airport. You emerge from the car park onto Wide Lane, turn right and follow it northwards towards Eastleigh. After 500 metres a gravel track leaves the road on the left going westward. This is the entrance to a park called Lakeside managed by Eastleigh Borough Council where there is also a car park. The area to the north is lower and in 500 metres you are passing to the south of some lakes. This track is called Doncaster Drove and on approaching the buildings on the south side of the lakeside the track returns to its original width of some 4 metres to become an unsurfaced leafy lane. At the western end a footbridge takes you over Monk's Brook onto a main road feeding towards the M27 to the south. The Concorde Club is to the north and to the south the IBM's Stoneham offices. Cross over with great care to take Stoneham Lane opposite westward. It is narrow with no footway, so be sure to walk facing oncoming traffic around the first bend where the lane heads south past St Nicolas church, North Stoneham, and on under the M27.

After the tunnel there is a stile on the left-hand side of the road. Cross it to follow a footpath which follows the south side of the motorway boundary fencing for 200 metres where it drops down to go through a tunnel under the road link to Portswood and Swaythling. Once out the other side turn sharp right up some steps to follow the field side of the highway boundary fencing going south. In 200 metres a field gate is reached in the boundary fencing. Do not go through it. Instead turn sharp left here and cross the field to pick up a path descending into the gulley containing Monk's Brook which is crossed by means of a footbridge into the area between the brook and the Southampton to Waterloo railway line. Here bear right to follow the brook along the east bank for 50 metres and up a path ascending to the railway line. The path crosses the tracks by means of a pedestrian crossing where it is necessary to take great care. After crossing a stile on the other side the path continues eastwards between fences to emerge once again on Wide Lane opposite the Ford factory to turn right.

Go south down Wide Lane taking the opportunity to cross over to the footway on the east side. In 400 metres turn left at the roundabout into Mansbridge Road, crossing over at the pedestrian crossing to continue along the south side heading east. In 500 metres the road bends right and the footway here is separated from the road and above it. Do not attempt to follow the carriageway around the bend as it is dangerous. Cross over Itchenside Close and continue to follow the segregated footway around the left-hand bend to arrive at the old Mans Bridge to join **The Itchen Way**.

Do not cross the bridge but turn left and go along the tarmac path underneath the new Mans Bridge. Once out onto the north side of the new bridge you have parkland ahead. The river Itchen bends eastwards from this point and going north is the silted up navigation. Continue along the east side of the parkland and if you have not spotted it yet the navigation is down in the bushes on your right. In the north-east corner a footpath leaves the green through the bushes to come out in 20 metres onto a cart track. Turn right on the track and go through an old metal field gate and across the site of the navigation and bend left following a path along the east side of the former navigation. Go north towards the M27 ahead.

At the motorway the path has been diverted eastward along a path enclosed on either side by fences for 400 metres to a bridge carrying the motorway over a tributary of the river Itchen. From here Gaters Mill can be seen off to the south-east across the meadows. Pass underneath the bridge and, once on the north side of the motorway, turn left and head west to reach the original north/south alignment of the path demarcated by staggered railings. At this point you are close to the south-eastern corner of Eastleigh Airport. Go north along the east bank of the silted up navigation, which is full of reeds and dry in summer. The path is through bushes and undergrowth with views east over the flood plain of the river Itchen. These fields are part of the Itchen Valley Country Park.

Although you will have to be observant to spot them, 700 metres from the motorway you will find the remains of Sandy Lock and, close to the point where you can see to the east the trees of Decoy Covert, is Decoy Pond Lock. When you reach the point where the covert is at its closest to the navigation there is a footpath link from the navigation to the footpath system within the Country Park. Continue along the navigation path to follow the Itchen Way.

With the Decoy Covert behind you, a wide vista over the fields to the east opens up. Some 1½ miles from the motorway just after another disused lock, you cross a track, the first noticeable break in the navigation path. Continue northwards and in 300 metres you reach the point where the path goes under the Eastleigh to Portsmouth railway line. Once on the north side of the railway line the path continues between fences, initially with fields on both sides, although that on the left is scheduled for industrial development. West Horton Farm and Allington Manor Farm are visible to the east. After 400 metres the path skirts to the east of a large sewage works, but mercifully the river Itchen and its meadows enhance the view to the east. Bishopstoke and Stoke Park Wood lie in the distance to the north-east. After some staggered railings you come out onto a private roadway.

Follow the roadway northwards and after 200 metres you can look down onto the confluence of the Barton river and the river Itchen to the right. The roadway then skirts around the east side of a small field and after 100 metres look for a footpath on the right leading almost immediately to a footbridge over the Barton river. After the bridge the path is north along the east side of the navigation now full of running water and wildlife. After 400 metres you reach the old Conegar Lock

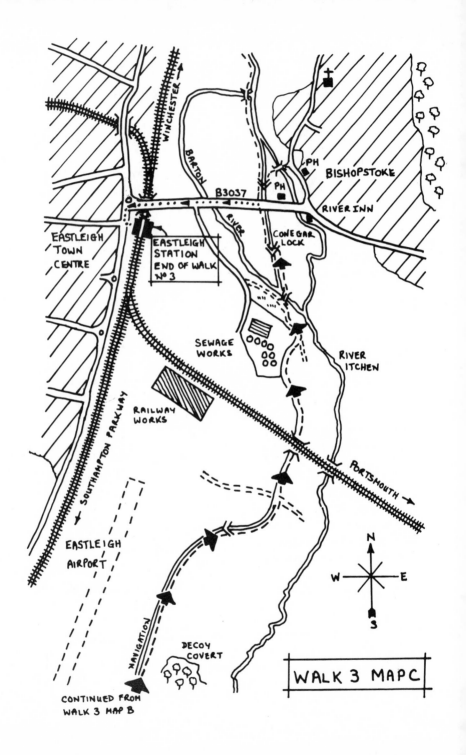

WALK 3 MAP C

which the path crosses by a footbridge to the west bank and continues north-north-west along the navigation. Five hundred metres from the lock the Bishopstoke Road (B3037) is reached. To the right is the Prince of Wales public house and, just beyond, The River Inn. The Itchen Way continues on the north side of the road. To follow **The Itchen Way** see the start of Walk Four.

To finish this walk turn left for ½ mile along the road over a bridge over the railway to the Eastleigh railway station. Once over the bridge bear down left to find the entrance to the station.

Historical Notes

Eastleigh: The Roman soldier travelling from Venta Belgarum (Winchester) to Clausentum (Bitterne) would have passed through thickly wooded hills which stretched down to an ill-drained marshy river valley through which the Itchen meandered. With clearance the Saxons would have found it ideal for improvement into pasture. It was referred to as 'Eastlea' in a survey attached to a charter in which King Athelstan granted land at North Stoneham to a military aid called Alfred in AD 932. In the Domesday Book it was called 'Estleie' and recorded as being held by Henry, the Treasurer. The settlement was described as one hide (50 hectares approx) although it was pointed out that it was twice that size in the reign of King Edward (1042–1066), plus ploughing land, meadows and woods for five hogs.

It was the coming of the railways to the valley which was to shatter the pattern of a thousand years of farming. An 1834 Act of Parliament authorised the construction of the London to Southampton line which opened in 1840. The Salisbury to Portsmouth and the Romsey to Salisbury lines followed in quick succession. Bishopstoke Junction was the meeting point and station. Dew Lane ran eastward past Little Eastley Farm to the north of the road and Great Eastley farm to the south. The beginnings of a town appeared with a cheese market, The

Junction Hotel, The Crown public house, Home Tavern and a smithy and a couple of rows of cottages: Tate's Terrace and Varna Terrace. From 200 inhabitants in 1851 it rose to over 1,000 by 1881.

In 1890/1 the London & South Western Railway opened a new carriage and wagon works at Eastleigh, employing 1,500 people and the Eastleigh Railway Institute was built. By 1897 the town of Eastleigh was well established, with housing constructed on a grid pattern from Derby Road to Leigh Road west of the Southampton Road and the railway. In 1903 the loco-engine cleaning and running sheds were transferred to Eastleigh from Northam, Southampton and in 1909/10 the locomotive engine works were transferred there from Nine Elms. All these job opportunities brought massive development and supporting trades, shops and services in its wake. The population rose from 3,582 in 1891, 15,613 in 1921 when the Pirelli General Cable Works was established, to 16,069 in 1931.

The first school was built in 1870 and by 1936 there were twelve schools. Administratively Eastleigh became an ecclesiastical parish in 1868. In 1892 a Local Government Board for Eastleigh was created with responsibility for drainage, sewerage, lighting and roads. In 1894 Eastleigh Urban District Council was established. Borough status was granted in 1936. In 1974 the present Eastleigh Borough Council was created on Local Government Reorganisation.

Eastleigh Museum: This small museum in High Street, Eastleigh has a display of the short history of the town and its environs, including many railway exhibits, photographs and plans.

At the museum a resource pack is available, entitled *Estllie from 1086 to 1936 – The Development of Eastleigh as a Community*. This joint publication of the Borough Council, Hampshire County Museum Service and Hampshire County Record Office contains a potted history of the town, five maps from 1791 to 1931 and extracts from historical records and old photographs.

Bishopstoke to Brambridge

Introduction: This extremely attractive circular walk in the valley floor between the urban areas of Eastleigh and Bishopstoke and on into beautiful countryside with water everywhere is a haven for ducks and swans so take some bread to feed them. The first half of the walk is along the Navigation from Bishopstoke by the side of playing fields and then past two disused locks through the meadows around Allbrook with the Waterloo to Weymouth railway line a constant companion. After reaching Brambridge with its historic house and garden centre it is back across the fields along the east ·side of the valley with views across the river Itchen. A steep ascent up a wooded slope leads to Stoke Common and then it's downhill past St Mary's church to return to Bishopstoke.

Distance: 4½ miles (7.2 km) of easy walking, this is an ideal walk for the family with plenty to keep children interested. The very young would need to be closely supervised because of the danger from waterways and road crossings. Walking boots recommended particularly during wet conditions for the return from Brambridge. The outward route is well surfaced and maintained.

Parking: To preserve continuity with Walk Three this walk starts at Bishopstoke where the navigation crosses the Bishopstoke road, but it is not possible to set down passengers or park at this location because of the volume of traffic using the road. There is street parking in the side streets of Bishopstoke to the east but please park sensibly not blocking private accessways.

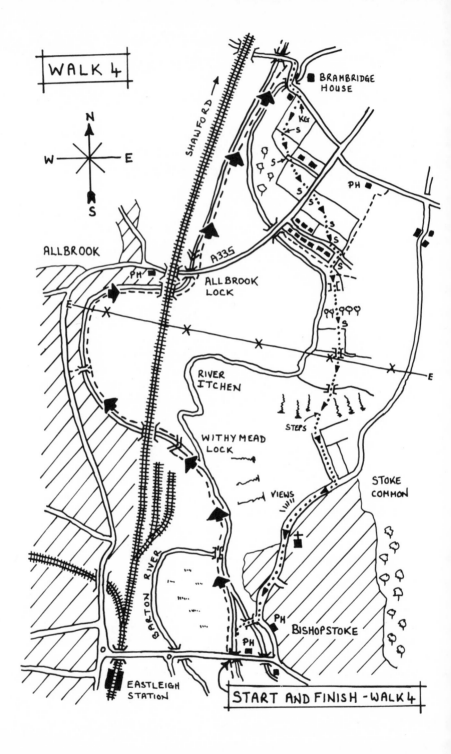

Itchen Way – Bishopstoke to Brambridge: This fourth stage of the Itchen Way follows the first half of Walk Four from the start on the B3037 until Brambridge where it then continues half way through Walk Five at page 44 for the section to Shawford.

The Walk: The start is ½ mile east of Eastleigh railway station on the B3037 where the navigation and the Itchen Way cross the road. Leave the road northwards along the west bank of the navigation, following the east side of the Bishopstoke Playing Fields. The path is tarmaced as far as a former lock reached after 200 metres. Ignore the footpath just before the lock on the right across a footbridge and continue on the west bank, passing to the left of some sluice gates and then over a small bridge over a sluice feeding the stream on the left. Five hundred and fifty metres from the B3037 the playing fields on the left end and you cross a bridge over a set of sluice gates controlling water entering Barton river. Continue north along the west bank of the river Itchen with a field to your left. After following the river around the eastern side of the second field you reach the point where the river Itchen forks to the right and the navigation commences a separate section to the left. The Itchen Way continues along the west bank of the navigation but almost immediately you reach the former Withymead Lock which you cross by a footbridge to the east bank. The Lock is near the sidings of the Eastleigh railway station. After 300 metres along the east side the former navigation and the footpath go under the main Bournemouth to Waterloo railway line.

The Itchen Way then follows the navigation for ⅔ mile in a loop with a segment-shaped field on the right and housing on the left. Soon you pass a bridge over the navigation which leads to Allbrook on the west bank. Continue northwards along the navigation's east bank under some high voltage electricity power lines, after which the navigation path bends round eastwards to go back under the Bournemouth to Waterloo railway line. It then bends sharply northwards to run close to the railway line. Almost immediately the A335 is reached. The

Victoria public house is under the railway bridge and 100 metres on the left. To continue the walk cross over the A335 and on the north side is the site of the Allbrook Lock and next to it a stile taking you onto the navigation path which continues to follow the east bank. After a further ½ mile of following the navigation path the river Itchen can be seen off to the east at the edge of some woods. Soon the footpath is sandwiched between the navigation and the river in a very pretty section for ½ mile until you reach the road at Brambridge. Those following **The Itchen Way** as a through route turn left here, cross over the road bridge over the navigation and turn immediately right to follow the west bank northwards, and turn to Walk Five on page 44.

To return to Bishopstoke on the circular walk turn right to follow the road, crossing over to the left-hand side to go carefully around the next right-hand bend past the entrance to Brambridge House and then cross over to the right-hand side before going over the narrow bridge over the river Itchen. Continue along the road past the entrance to Brambridge Park Garden Centre and just beyond Bridge Cottage there is a kissing gate on the right taking you out into the field to the south of the road. Head south across the field to a stile in the southern boundary fence near the south-western corner. Head south across the next field towards a stile next to a field gate in the south-eastern corner. Once over the stile you are into a small entrance lane serving Mallard Cottage. Leave the lane almost immediately on the right over a stile into the field to the south which is crossed diagonally southwards to a stile in the south-eastern boundary fence leading out onto the A335. Cross over the road and over a stile on the other side to continue on a path heading across a field in the same direction as in the field before the road. Pick up a stile midway along the southern boundary. The path continues diagonally across the next small field in the same direction to another stile midway along the southern boundary of that field which takes you out onto an unsurfaced gravel track called Wardle Road.

Turn left along Wardle Road for 50 metres to pick up a path going south on the right (opposite another going north) at a stile. Once over the stile you are in a narrow field leading south towards the meadows of the river Itchen. Once you have reached the point in the field level with the bottom of the garden of the property on your right and dropped down slightly into the meadows, you are at a crossroads in the footpath network: one going west to the A335, one going east over a stile into some woods, and another which you should take going straight ahead south across the flat meadows. In 40 metres you cross a small bridge over a water meadow channel, 200 metres further on you cross another indistinct water channel marked by a line of trees where there is no footbridge. Another 150 metres and a stile is crossed in an east/west fence. Continue south across a footbridge over a stream leading into the river Itchen and pass to the left of a large electricity pylon. From here you can look across the meadows to Allbrook where you went under the same line going along the navigation. From here you continue southwards, passing to the right of a single electricity pole to find a footbridge over a small stream leading into some woods. This steeply wooded bank is called Stoke Common Copse and the path climbs up it going south and bearing slightly to the right. It is a two minute climb to the top and there are steps up the last 50 metres. At the top bear right to pick up a path continuing southwards between fences to come out onto Church Road, Stoke Common.

Turn right and head south along the road to a telephone box at the brow of the hill and cross over to the footway on the other side. Follow Church Road downhill for almost ½ mile, passing on the way some excellent views westwards across the river Itchen, then Mount Hospital, St Mary's church and a general stores for refreshment. After a slight bend in the road to the right at the junction with Spring Lane and then a bend to the left, a recreation ground appears on your left. Before going around the next left-hand bend, cross over to the right-hand side of the road where you will find Oak Bank Road. Turn right down it and it turns into a tarmac footpath leading to a footbridge over the river Itchen. Once on the other side the path bends left to pass the sluice gates you met earlier in the walk and then to turn right over a footbridge onto the navigation path where you should turn left and go south to the Bishopstoke Road where this walk started.

Historical Notes

'A Protest Meeting at Bishopstoke' is the title of Occasional Paper No 15 published by the Eastleigh and District Local History Society. It records the details of a meeting which took place on 30th November 1905 to protest against the demolition of the old Parish Church at Bishopstoke and the levelling of the graves in the churchyard the site of which is on the south side of Oak Bank Road near the end of this walk.

'Memories of Old Eastleigh and Bishopstoke' by Maureen Westwood and published by the author in 1985 recounts the memories of some residents illustrated with many old photographs, study of which will make the walk around Bishopstoke all the more interesting.

Shawford to Brambridge

Introduction: This is a circular walk full of interest. After an energetic climb from the car park to the war memorial on Shawford Down there is a superb view around the adjacent hills and north to Winchester. Then one of the many contrasts occurs as the walk enters the luxurious Southdown Estate with its quality homes of distinction before emerging into the older village of Otterbourne. Then it is over a low ridge through fields to the site of the old St Matthew's church and down to the Itchen Navigation at Brambridge. Turning north the walk follows the Navigation through the meadows of the central Itchen valley with splendid scenery all the way back to the village of Shawford.

This is an ideal walk for those dependent on public transport as there is an hourly train service to Shawford Station.

Distance: 4 miles (6.4 km) of easy walking but care is required on the lane near Brambridge because of vehicular traffic. The navigation path and the fields can be muddy in wet weather so walking boots are recommended.

Parking: Available free at the Shawford Down Car Park but because of the popularity of the Down, particularly at weekends, the area does get quite congested on occasion.

Itchen Way – Brambridge to Shawford: The fifth stage of the Itchen Way starts at the halfway point in this walk at Brambridge (page 44) and continues up the Navigation to the Bridge Hotel at Shawford from where the Itchen Way continues at the beginning of Walk Six.

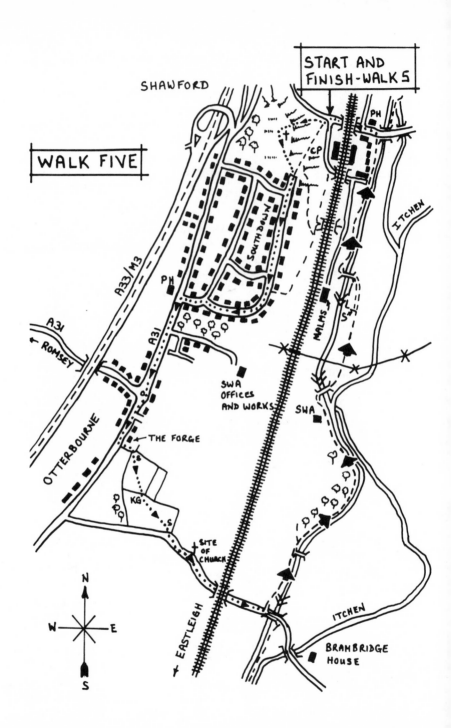

The Walk: The start of this walk is at the Shawford Down Car Park which is located immediately to the west of the Shawford Railway Station and takes the form of a linear layby off a minor roadway running south from Shawford Road. First to enjoy the spectacular views from the top of the down climb up towards the stone war memorial cross visible above. Continue up even higher and you will have a view across the valley in an arc, incorporating Colden Common to the south, both sections of Twyford to the east, and St Catharine's Hill and Winchester including the cathedral to the north.

Then head south across the open grassland, not losing height, to pick up a narrow tarmac pathway which ascends from the road near the railway station in a gulley marked by a line of trees and bushes. Follow it right, south-westwards, entering a belt of trees and into the Southdown Estate, an area of extremely well appointed properties. In 1899 a syndicate of property developers bought 135 acres from the Ecclesiastical Commissioners to promote this prestige estate. After leaving the downland you follow a pathway for 100 metres to join Southdown Road. Head south along the road past houses with lovely landscaped gardens. After ¼ mile you pass the road Cross Way on the right and after another 300 metres a more modern section of Southdown Road turns sharp right within an area of newer houses. After another 300 metres, Southdown Road becomes Grove Road and continues west. At the junction with Fairfield Road turn left along Grove Road to join the Winchester road opposite the Captain Barnard Free House.

Turn left along the Winchester Road (A31) downhill for ½ mile along the left-hand side of the road. This was a Roman Road forming a link between Venta Belgarum (Winchester) and Clausentum (Bitterne) and the roman port at Nursling. On the way down you pass the entrance to Sparrowgrove and then the roundabout where the A31 goes right towards Romsey. Continue straight on downhill towards Chandlers Ford past the entrance to Oak Wood Avenue on your left, a petrol filling station on the right, and across the Otter Bourne which rises in Poleshole Spring 150 metres to the west. After passing Brooklyn Close on the left you reach the Old Forge restaurant where

43

there was a female blacksmith in the early 19th century called Betsy Comely.

The ancient route to Brambridge is now to be followed. Turn into the car park serving the south side of the restaurant and at the far end, in the south-eastern corner, is a stile taking you out into a field to the south-east. You are now in the north-west corner of the field and the path goes diagonally across to the south-eastern corner. The Southern Water Sparrowgrove Works are visible off to the north-east. At the south-eastern corner of the field you cross the crest of a slight ridge through a kissing gate and into the field beyond. Bear left and down to the south-eastern corner of the field; leave it via a stile adjacent to a field gate to join the road between Otterbourne and Brambridge. Turn left and head east along the road, taking great care. At the first bend on the left is the site of the old St Matthew's church which was erected in the 13th century. It was replaced by the new church of the same name in Otterbourne when it opened in 1838. The nave of the old church was demolished in 1842 and the chancel in 1970 but the gravestones remain.

One hundred metres further on the road goes under the railway line. In another 100 metres you reach the road bridge over the navigation and the route which we used in Walk Four. Do not cross the bridge but turn left to follow **The Itchen Way** and the navigation path northwards along the west bank. Soon you are passing another old lock where there are some large sluice gates. After a small vehicular road bridge across the navigation on the right and then a stile on the left (both of which you ignore to stay on the west bank), the navigational path bends north-eastwards and then bends north with a beautiful rural aspect to the east across flat meadows with a backdrop of the downs between Colden Common and Twyford. Then the navigation turns distinctly north-westwards and ½ mile from Brambridge you arrive at a Southern Water Authority plant house and outlet into the waterway at the confluence of the navigation to the left and the river to the right. Fifty metres beyond the SWA building, turn right over a vehicular bridge over the navigation near the former College

Mead Lock now forming a picturesque waterfall. Follow the farm track northwards which is fenced on both sides and runs through flat sheep pastures. As you pass under some high voltage electricity cables you can see Twyford church slightly to the right. At the end of the straight, at a field gate, turn left over a stile to follow a footpath between fences leading to the navigation near the former Malms Lock with Malms House in the background. The house was built after the First World War by Alfred Bowker who was involved in the Southdown development. Follow the path right, north along the east bank of the navigation. As you approach farm buildings on the left you cross over a stile on the navigation path to rejoin the continuation of the farm track that you were walking along earlier. Cross over the navigation by a farm road bridge and immediately turn right over a stile to follow the west bank.

The crystal clear waters are elevated above the pastures to the east and are the regular haunt of wildfowl and swans. Concealed in a cutting to the west is the Bournemouth to Waterloo railway line. Between the railway line and the navigation is a small tarmaced road which the navigation path joins briefly after 300 metres where there is a tunnel under the now elevated railway. Continue to follow the navigation rather than the roadway and in 400 metres you will find yourself heading towards the right-hand end of a row of cottages at right angles to the navigation. Leave the linear field to go through a kissing gate and onto a tarmaced pathway going to the right of the aforementioned cottages, continuing along the side of the navigation. There is a line of houses between the navigation path and the railway line and Shawford Station. In 200 metres you reach the B3386 between Shawford and Twyford. To follow the through route on **The Itchen Way**, continue northwards by turning right over the road bridge and immediately left along the east bank of the navigation. Turn to Walk Six on page 47.

To return to the start of this walk, turn left along the road past Shawford Post Office on the left and the Bridge Hotel on the right following the road under the railway to the Shawford Down Car Park. The railway station was built in 1882 and was used as a set for part of a remake of *Brief Encounter* featuring Sophia Loren and Richard Burton.

Historical Notes

The Captain Barnard Free House is named after Captain Barnard who commanded a party of Roundheads billeted in Compton in the Civil War. In 1645 he intervened to prevent his men eating a feast including the ale prepared by Mrs Goldfinch of Manor Farm, Compton to celebrate the birth of her son. At his request the son was christened with his name and Barnard Goldfinch is buried in Compton churchyard.

Brambridge House: This was the home of the Catholic Welles family for three and a half centuries. Swithun Welles was hanged in front of his London home with a priest, after being arrested in 1591 for celebrating mass. In 1763 Henry Welles left the house and estate to his cousin, Walter Smythe. Walter Smythe's daughter, Maria Fitzherbert, from 1784 had a famous love affair and secret marriage in 1785 to George, Prince of Wales, later George IV.

Shawford to Winchester

Introduction: It is the sweeping views from the hills around Winchester which are a feature of this walk. From the Shawford Down Car Park it is up the Itchen Navigation with Twyford church off to the east until Hockley traffic lights. Then along the edge of the water meadows with an optional detour to climb up St Catharine's Hill with its Iron Age encampment from where historic Winchester can be seen laid out below. On reaching Winchester and its famous college the walk turns south-west to visit the Hospital of St Cross. Leaving the valley behind, it is up Whiteside Lane to Badger Farm, another good viewpoint over Winchester. Following ancient bridle roads overlooking Compton End the walk then turns south to get views across to Cranbury Park before entering the select residential estates of Yarners Green and the Southdown Estate. Finishing via the top of Shawford Down, from where most of the walk can be seen below, completes this circular tour. This walk is especially good at dawn or in the changing light of evening.

There is an hourly train service to Shawford Station which makes this walk ideal for those dependent on public transport.

Distance: About 7½ miles (12.1 km) of pleasant walking. Walking boots required because the navigation path can be muddy in wet weather. No strenuous climbs apart from the optional ascent of St Catharine's Hill where there are many steps.

Parking: Available free at the Shawford Down Car Park but because of the popularity of the Down at weekends the area does, on occasion, get quite congested.

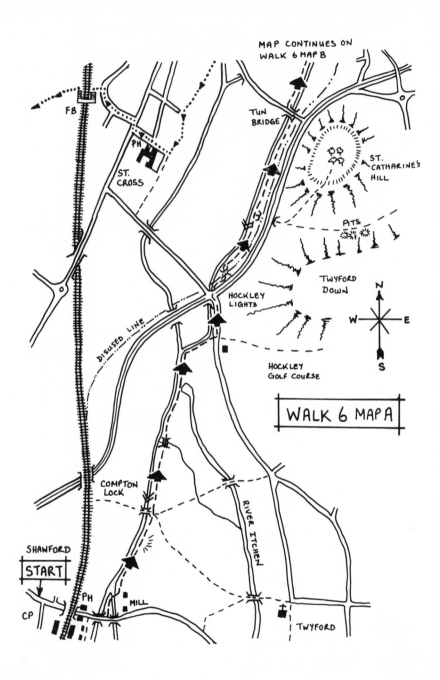

Itchen Way – Shawford to Winchester: This sixth stage of the Itchen Way starts close to the start of this walk at the Bridge Hotel, Shawford and continues northwards along the Itchen Navigation until Wharf Hill at the edge of Winchester. Then turn to Walk Eight at page 63.

The Walk: From the car park return to the Shawford Road and turn right along it to head east past the station and under the railway line and past the Bridge Hotel. Go over the road bridge across the navigation and turn sharp left to follow the east bank northwards. Immediately to the right is a disused mill and the mill race leading to it which you cross after 50 metres via a small footbridge. The mill was last used in the Second World War and a date stone implies it was built in 1795.

As you begin to leave Shawford behind, Twyford church appears across the meadows to the right. It was rebuilt in 1876 when twelve large Druid stones were discovered which now are in the foundations of the tower. Its façade is alternate bands of brick and flint. An earlier church was mentioned in the Domesday Book and there has been an unbroken line of Vicars since 1301. After ¼ mile you reach the remains of Compton Lock where there is a footbridge taking a path west to Compton. On the right is the path back across the fields to Twyford leading directly to the church. Ahead the Itchen Way continues north on the east bank towards Hockley. After ½ mile you cross a small footbridge over an overflow channel. Three hundred metres further on you will see the river Itchen on your right getting closer and then you come to Tumbling Bay, a circular pond-like feature where water from the navigation discharges into it to form the river. Continue north on the east bank of what is now a combined navigation and river Itchen for only another 200 metres. The river bears left and the navigation heads right, north-east. Follow the old towpath on the navigation which is a silted up relic, to come out onto the main road between the Winchester by-pass and Twyford, opposite the Hockley golf course.

49

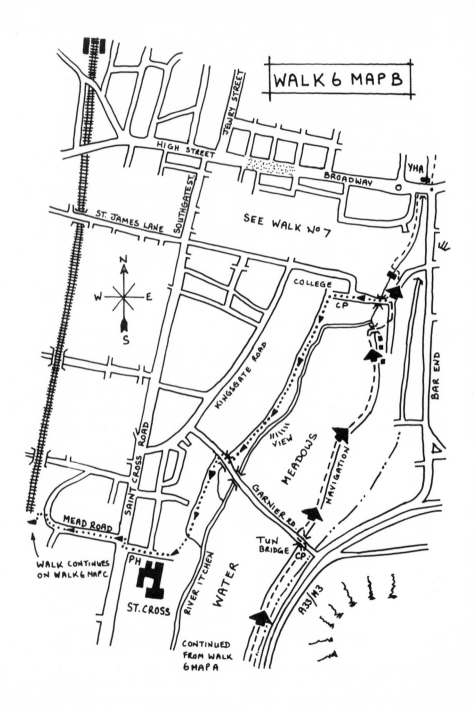

WALK 6 MAP B

YHA

HIGH STREET

JEWRY STREET

SOUTHGATE ST.

BROADWAY

ST. JAMES LANE

SEE WALK Nº 7

N
W E
S

COLLEGE

CP

KINGSGATE ROAD

BAR END

SAINT CROSS ROAD

VIEW

MEADOWS

NAVIGATION

MEAD ROAD

GARNIER RD.

TUN
BRIDGE

CP

WALK CONTINUES
ON WALK 6 MAP C

PH

RIVER ITCHEN

WATER

A33/M3

ST. CROSS

CONTINUED
FROM WALK
6 MAP A

Cross over the road and follow the roadside path northwards to the Hockley traffic lights. The proposed construction of the M3 will make a mess here so look out for diversions. (The Twyford to Hockley road will be diverted just north of the point where you join it. It will run further west on the site of the navigation under the M3 where you will then have to turn right to pick up the original route.) Until then take care and cross over the dual carriageway via the traffic island and immediately turn to the right to follow a tarmac footway northwards along the west side of the dual carriageway, heading on the pathway into some trees and under a disused railway line via a tunnel. Immediately on the other side you will find the navigation. Turn to go northwards along a path sandwiched between the navigation on the west and the disused railway embankment to the east.

After 400 metres you reach a large disused lock, part of which has been reconstructed as a weir which controls the water level upstream into Winchester. Immediately on the right after the lock there is a tunnel under the dual carriageway and former railway which takes the walker out into a picturesque valley. The dual carriageway will be closed and landscaped after the construction of the M3 which should greatly improve the environment at this side of St Catharine's Hill. There is a footpath ahead along the valley floor which goes past some chalk cuttings and some mounds, the latter being the common graves of the local victims of the Plague of 1666. There is also a path up the side of St Catharine's Hill with plenty of steps leading to the oval ramparts of a 23 acre Iron Age fort with a major north-eastern entrance. There is a panoramic view of Winchester from the earthworks which make a rewarding walk.

Return back under the tunnel to the navigation path and continue northwards. After 100 metres there is the option of following the bank or using a wider path above it from which there are good views across the meadows to St Cross. Both paths merge just before an unofficial car park next to Tun Bridge which carries Garnier Road and the Itchen Way over the navigation. Turn left over the bridge and turn sharp right to

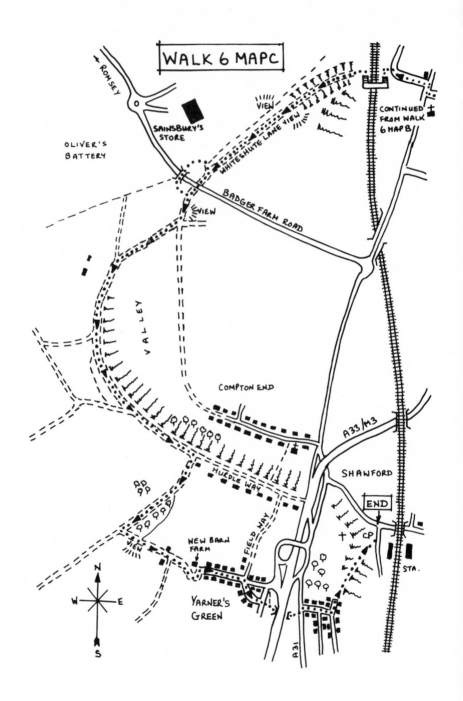

follow the west bank of the navigation, with water meadows to the west and Palmer Field playing fields to the east. After a couple of sluices releasing navigation waters into the water meadows you reach the first of the houses in Winchester. This route takes you directly into the heart of the city along a green corridor.

Once upstream of the rowing club premises on the opposite bank, the path crosses over a brick hump-backed bridge over the navigation to the east bank again where you leave it, following a footpath for 30 metres to join the narrow Domum Road. Turn north along it for 50 metres to reach a secondary road. The road ahead is called Wharf Hill and **The Itchen Way** leaves this walk to follow it northwards. Continue from the start of Walk Eight.

To continue this walk turn left and go west on the road called College Walk, crossing a bridge over the river Itchen almost immediately. Follow the footway for a further 100 metres to where the road turns sharp right. Here continue straight on along a route signposted to St Cross via the water meadows. Initially you pass through a gravelly surfaced car park and reach a private entrance to Winchester College which was founded in 1382 to train scholars for the Church by William of Wykeham, Bishop of Winchester from 1366 to 1404. Here turn sharp left to follow a gravel path heading south along the east bank of a picturesque little stream. In 100 metres you are sandwiched between the river Itchen on the left and the little stream on the right. Continue to follow the gravel path next to the small stream for ½ mile, ignoring the footbridges over to the playing fields to the west and admiring the excellent views east to the Iron Age fort on St Catharine's Hill, until you reach Garnier Road again. Turn right and cross over the bridge over the little stream and turn sharp left to continue along another gravel path, this time on the western side of the stream with yet another rivulet on the right.

Ignore the footbridge which leads across the stream on the right into Cripstead Lane and continue south along the gravel track through a kissing gate. Go over a sluice taking the rivulet under the footpath and you enter a field with the ancient St

53

Cross complex ahead, surrounded by a stone wall capped with tiles. On reaching the wall turn right to follow it west along a track, to leave the field via a kissing gate next to a white field gate. Although there is a declaration by the Trustees of the Hospital of St Cross that this is not a right-of-way, it is a well used track which leads to the entrance to the chapel and hospital which is open to the public with a modest admission charge.

To continue the walk, head west along a private tarmac roadway to arrive on the main Saint Cross Road and The Bell Inn. Cross over Saint Cross Road, using the pedestrian crossing if it is busy, and head up the road opposite called Mead Road which ascends for 300 metres past Hubert Road. At the first right-hand bend you will find a footbridge which will take you over the main Bournemouth to Waterloo railway line.

Once on the other side of the railway, turn sharp left to follow a track through undergrowth and into a sunken lane. This substantial pathway commences a long and steady climb. In 400 metres you get the chance to look back across to St Cross and St Catharine's Hill with a view towards Chilcomb. Continue along the sunken pathway and after another couple of hundred metres it would be worth taking any pathway on the right to come out onto the ridge where there are magnificent views down across Winchester. The cathedral and South-gate church, the home of the Hampshire Records Office, and the County Council's Castle complex stand out clearly. Having admired the view return to the sunken pathway which is called Whiteshute Lane and continue south-westwards. Nearly a mile from Mead Road you will begin to glimpse the Sainsbury's superstore off to your right, and then the path suddenly reaches a chalk road coming from the right leading ahead and down to the main Badger Farm Road. Cross over taking care and up the chalk road on the other side, continuing in a south-westerly direction. If the Badger Farm Road is likely to pose a problem there is an alternative route via a footbridge slightly to the north-west.

Three hundred metres from the Badger Farm Road along the chalk road and you are enjoying, at a crossroads of tracks, panoramic views towards Winchester to the north-east, Twyford to the south-east and to the south is Compton Down. Fork right, following the alignment of two sets of electricity lines. It is a farm trackway heading south-west which begins to descend gently into a valley. You can see ahead the track climbing up the other side. Off to the right is the housing estate called Oliver's Battery. In 500 metres you reach the bottom of the valley and a bridleway coming from the housing estate now to the right and behind you. At this junction bear left to leave the electricity cables, continuing to follow a well defined farm track. Initially it is fairly level but then it begins to climb towards the escarpment ahead. Half way up you reach another junction of several tracks where you should continue to climb, but bear left along the ridge to enjoy a magnificent view down across Compton End with Twyford church visible across the Itchen valley beyond. Close to the highest point of the ridge you meet yet another junction of paths. Continue south-east, upwards and bearing left along the top of the escarpment on a more substantial unsurfaced roadway.

St Catharine's Hill dominates the centre of the view northwards and the track levels out and begins to descend for over ½ mile. As the trees on the left block out the view of Compton below and just before the first house on the right, turn right up another unsurfaced roadway to go south-westwards. After a short climb it begins to descend slightly, initially with fields on both sides and then along the right-hand or western side of a woodland. At the south-western corner of the woodland, although the track continues on downhill towards the hamlet of Silkstead, turn left to follow the main farm road south-eastwards towards New Barn Farm. Across on the ridge to the south are the grounds of Cranbury Park, although the house is not visible from this side. After passing between a pair of outlying barns, continue eastward where another major farm-road goes south. The roadway passes to the right or the south side of the farmhouse, following the brick boundary wall and then bears left and then right onto Shepherds Lane which is tarmaced. Continue east along it among another fine area of prestigious houses called Yarner's Green. Three hundred metres short of the A33 (and intended M3) you reach a crossroads in the tarmac roads. Field Way is to the left, but turn right to follow another minor road that bends eastwards again towards the A33. On reaching a T-junction, go straight across and descend some steps to follow a tarmac pathway going through an underpass under the main road. On emerging at the other side bear left, cross over the Winchester Road (A31) via a central reservation and go straight on down Southdown Road. Follow it eastward past Fairfield Road on the right until you get to the point where Southdown Road turns right southwards. Turn left here, following a path going north which leads out onto Shawford Down. The direct route to the car park is to follow the tarmac pathway descending steadily northeastwards, most of the way in a gulley. You may prefer to go north along the ridge to the war memorial cross to enjoy the views before descending east to the car park below.

Historical Notes

The Hospital of St Cross: Henry de Blois, grandson of William the Conqueror, Bishop of Winchester and brother of King Stephen, founded in 1136 what is claimed to be Britain's oldest existing charitable institution to provide a home for men too old and poor to defend themselves. Its elderly inhabitants are dressed distinctively in cloaks and hats. On entering the complex you are initially in an outer quadrangle with toilets on your right and the Beaufort Tower ahead, named after Henry Beaufort who was Bishop of Winchester in the first half of the 15th century. At the base of the tower is an archway where the ticket office is located in the Porter's Lodge. Through the archway is the inner quadrangle with the Chapel of St Cross ahead, with to its right a gap where the south wing was demolished in 1788 because it was in disrepair. The Brothers' flats are on the right with their distinctive chimneys. Immediately on the right next to the tower are some steps which take you up to the Brothers' Hall and Kitchen which are open to the public. To the left is the 16th century Ambulatory or cloister from which access can be obtained into a pretty and peaceful walled garden complete with ornamental pond.

St Catharine's Hill: Catharine was the only daughter and heiress of the King of Egypt in the early 4th century. When he died she was just 14 and she became queen in Alexandria, declining wedlock. Having been converted to the Christian faith by a hermit, the Roman Emperor Maxentius sent pagan philosophers to pervert her, but she converted them to Christianity instead. Enraged, the emperor ordered the martyrdom of the philosophers and ordered Catharine to be broken on the wheel, but through 'divine intervention' the wheel broke. Alas this did not stop her being scourged and beheaded. Her grave was found five centuries later on Mount Sinai where there is now a monastery, hence she was a popular subject when naming hilltop chapels.

St Catharine's Hill was occupied between 500 and 100 BC. Beneath a plantation of mature trees on the top is the buried remains of St Catharine's chapel which was destroyed between 1538 and 1540. The area was excavated between 1925 and 1928.

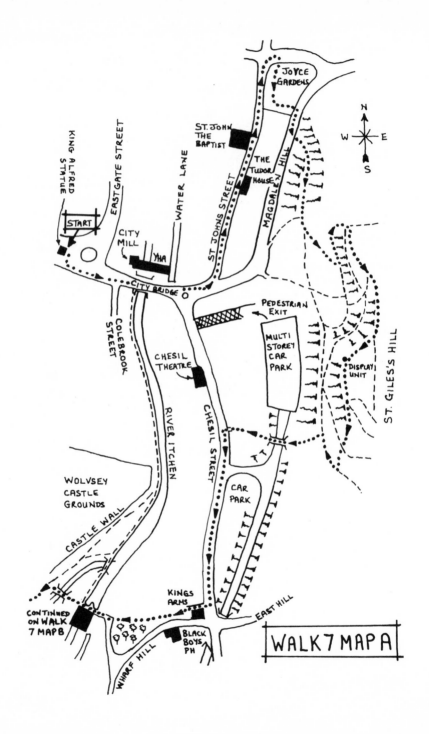

WALK 7 MAP A

Winchester City

Introduction: This tour of the historic city of Winchester provides an opportunity to explore and allows the long distance walker to put down his rucksack and have a rest. The three maps are sufficiently detailed to make a description of the walk unnecessary. However, any visit to the city should commence with a call at the Information Centre in the Guildhall to collect background guides and maps. There are also guided walks in the summer months.

Historical Notes

Winchester: Two Iron Age forts on either side of the Itchen at St Catharine's Hill and Oram's Arbour in the north-western sector of the present city marked the start of the history of this settlement. The Romans established the city Venta Belgarum using Clausentum as its port. It became the fifth largest in the British occupation and a centre for the Belgae. On the departure of the Romans at the end of the 4th century a period of decay set in, but soon it became the centre of Saxon influence and a capital for the kings of Wessex. Sacked by the Vikings in AD 860, it then became the centre of learning and administration for King Alfred's kingdom which he had secured by force in AD 878.

Ecclesiastically the conversion of the Saxon kings to Christianity in AD 635 led to the building of the 'Old Minster' in AD 648 whose foundations are marked by stones immediately to the east of the current cathedral. Cenwalh, King of Wessex, transferred his bishopric there in AD 662. King Alfred and his queen had the Nuns' Minster built, his son Edward the Elder

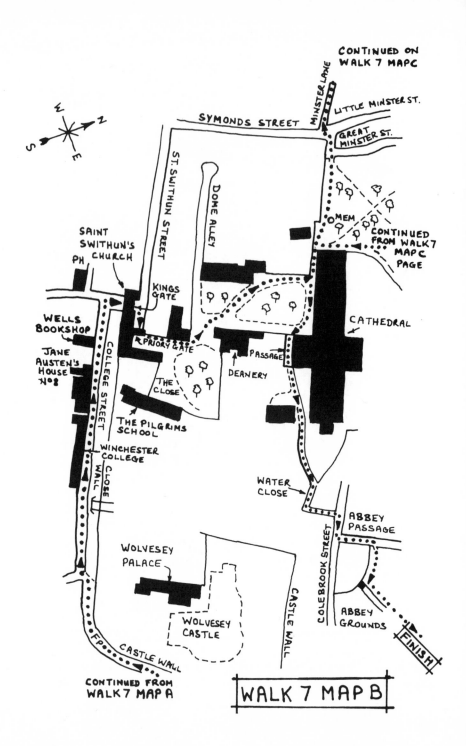

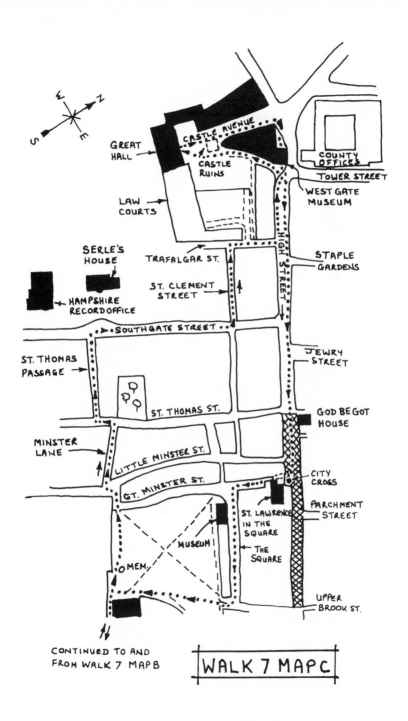

CONTINUED TO AND
FROM WALK 7 MAP B

WALK 7 MAP C

had the New Minster built, which transferred to Hyde, to the north-east of the city in 1110.

The surrender of the city to William, Duke of Normandy, in 1066 marked the start of the Norman era during which the Domesday Book was compiled in Winchester. A large castle was built on the site of part of the Saxon town near the present law courts and the cathedral was established and dedicated in 1093. In 1141 much of Winchester was destroyed in a battle which led to the defeat of the forces of Empress Matilda by those of Stephen I in a decisive battle for the English throne. Prosperity came with the St Giles's Fair and the pilgrimage to St Swithin's tomb.

In the Reformation of 1536 to 1540 many treasures were lost including Hyde Abbey and that of St Mary's. In an era of religious intolerance Mary Tudor married Philip II of Spain in the cathedral in 1554. During the Civil War, in 1642 the cathedral was desecrated and many manuscripts lost and in 1645 the castle and the city were captured by Oliver Cromwell's forces.

Its famous residents have included Isaac Walton in Dome Alley and Jane Austen at Number 8 College Street. Both were buried in the cathedral, as was the poet John Keats. Mary Sumner, the founder of the Mothers Union, lived at Number 1 The Close during the early days of that organisation.

Today Winchester is still the administrative centre for Hampshire County Council and a regional base for many organisations, with a prosperous shopping centre and a wealth of places of interest for the tourist.

Winchester to Abbots Worthy

Introduction: From King Alfred's Statue in the centre of Winchester this circular walk goes past the City Mill and north out of Winchester. It passes quickly into open country with fishing lakes, marsh and water meadows. An attractive riverside path goes under the A33 and continues north-east to the charming house at Fulling Mill. Then, after crossing a number of water channels, the well defined path crosses a quaint bridge over the Itchen to the pretty village of Abbots Worthy. The return route is along the other side of the Itchen via Kings Worthy and the church of St Mary, Abbotts Barton and the North Walls recreation ground. There is an optional stroll around the nature trail in the Winnall Moors Nature Reserve. There is much to attract the bird watcher and the quiet, patient observer.

Distance: About 5 miles (8.2 km) of very easy walking, but could be very muddy in winter in parts.

Parking: Best done on a Sunday when parking is easier in Winchester. There is long-term parking in the Chesil Street multi-storey car park close to the start.

Itchen Way – Winchester to Abbots Worthy: This seventh stage of the Itchen Way begins by taking the short link set out below from Wharf Hill reached in Walk Six to Bridge Street to pick up Walk Eight near the start. It then continues following Walk Eight until the crossing of the Itchen and the entrance to Abbots Worthy. Then continue near the start of Walk Nine on page 73.

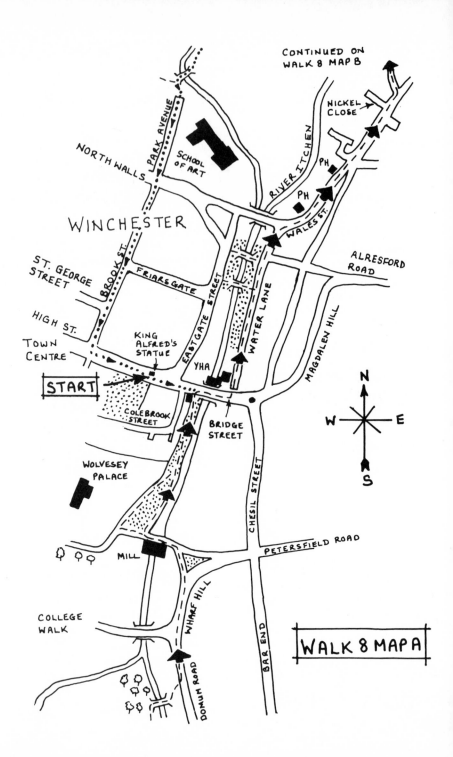

Itchen Way Link from Walk Six: From the junction of Wharf Hill and Domum Road (see map page 64) continue northwards along Wharf Hill for 100 metres and then bear left to recross what is now the river Itchen near the mill converted into flats. Immediately turn right to follow the river northwards along the west bank through a parkland setting. You join Bridge Street opposite the Winchester City Mill. The city of Winchester and King Alfred's statue are to the left.

The Walk: The start is King Alfred's statue in the Broadway (see map opposite), that famous bronze statue on two blocks of Cornish granite erected in 1901 to a King of Wessex who made Winchester his capital. Go east past the roundabout and along Bridge Street to pick up the Itchen Way, over the bridge next to Winchester City Mill and then left into Water Lane, where you will find the entrance to the City Mill Youth Hostel.

Continuing along Water Lane, after 50 metres bear left to follow the tarmac path along the riverside park. Ignore two footbridges over the river. After the second, cross over the road to the right-hand side and go round a bend. The new Durngate Bridge leads westward, but continue instead north-east along Wales Street past The Sun Inn and then The First In – Last Out public house. You then meet the first buildings in the Winnall Trading Estate. Having passed the junction of Wales Street and Easton Lane (really a continuation of the same road) and the industrial units in Nickel Close, turn left down a narrow, partially tarmaced road serving some bungalows on its north-eastern side. The road ends in 200 metres where there is a stile between two field gates leading on in the same direction into a long linear field. (See map page 66) There are a large number of lakes and water channels in the meadows to the north-west frequented by Winchester and Eastleigh Fishing Club members.

At the northern end of the linear field cross over a stile into a second linear field and now there is the alignment of a disused railway line on the right and, beyond, a trading estate. At the north end of the field you will find another stile followed quickly by another. Follow the well defined path northwards

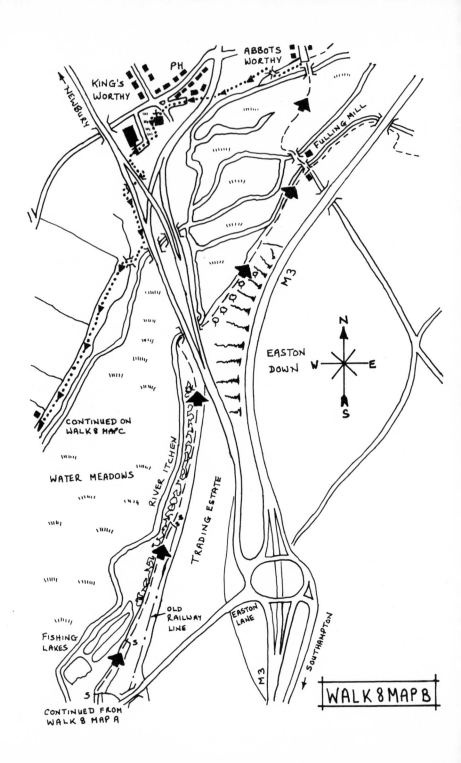

KING'S WORTHY

PH

ABBOTS WORTHY

NEWBURY

FULLING MILL

M3

EASTON DOWN

N
W E
S

CONTINUED ON WALK 8 MAP C

RIVER ITCHEN

WATER MEADOWS

TRADING ESTATE

OLD RAILWAY LINE

EASTON LANE

M3

SOUTHAMPTON

FISHING LAKES

S

S

S

CONTINUED FROM WALK 8 MAP A

WALK 8 MAP B

through woodland and undergrowth with the river Itchen meadows to the west, and industrial buildings to the east. After ¼ mile you begin to have views across the meadows towards Headbourne Worthy and to hear the traffic noise from the Winchester to Newbury road. Soon you reach the river Itchen and turn right following a riverside path under the bridges carrying first the northbound and then the southbound carriageways. Continue upstream along the edge of the field beyond. You can now see the M3 off to the right. The path does not follow the riverbank after 100 metres but joins a well defined argricultural farm track along the base of the escarpment of Easton Down. After another 400 metres you reach a field sandwiched between the meadows to the north-west and the embankment of the M3 to the east. Follow the western side of the field and, at the north-western end, pass to the left of some domestic garages and turn left to join the entrance road and bridge to the splendid house set in water gardens at Fulling Mill.

Pass directly in front of the house, respecting the occupants' privacy, and over the footbridge over the second water channel to follow a narrow footpath between fences. Bear right over the third water channel along a well defined track crossing the meadows and marshes to Abbots Worthy. Just before you reach the village you cross a major watercourse by a three arched bridge to end up on tarmac road. Immediately on the right is a metal kissing gate marking the continuation of **The Itchen Way** where those on the through route should leave and continue from the start of Walk Nine.

To continue this walk, turn left to follow the south side of a minor rivulet, with a house to the north and the meadows of the Itchen to the south. The path is between metal railings and the rivulet for 200 metres and then a footbridge takes the path over the rivulet. On the other side of the bridge take the left-hand of two side gates and continue west along the north side of the Itchen marshland under an avenue of trees. After 300 metres you ascend to reach the edge of the A33, the road between Winchester and Basingstoke. Cross over via the central reservation taking great care and follow the continuation

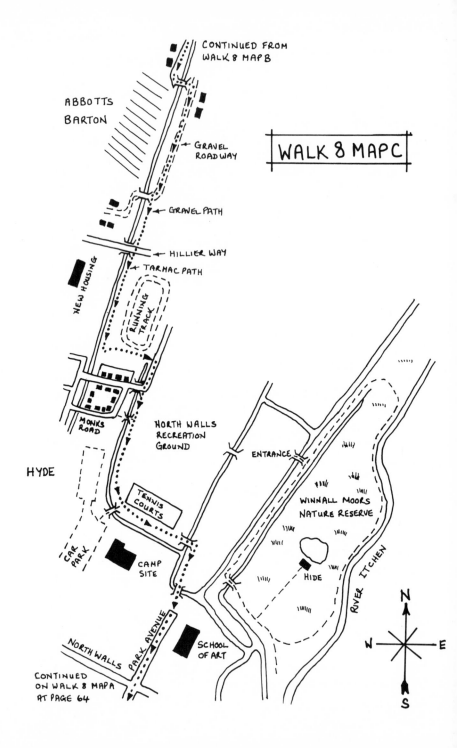

CONTINUED FROM
WALK 8 MAP B

ABBOTTS
BARTON

GRAVEL
ROADWAY

GRAVEL PATH

HILLIER WAY

TARMAC PATH

NEW HOUSING

RUNNING
TRACK

WALK 8 MAP C

MONKS
ROAD

NORTH WALLS
RECREATION
GROUND

ENTRANCE

HYDE

TENNIS
COURTS

WINNALL MOORS
NATURE RESERVE

CAR
PARK

CAMP
SITE

HIDE

RIVER ITCHEN

NORTH WALLS

PARK AVENUE

SCHOOL
OF ART

CONTINUED
ON WALK 8 MAP A
AT PAGE 64

N
W   E
S

of the path through a side gate to the left of Eversley Cottage opposite. The path is defined by a line of paving slabs for a short distance and then arrives on a gravel road in the village of Kings Worthy. Continue straight on along the gravel road in the direction of the tower of St Mary's church ahead.

Pass immediately along the north side of the church, turning left on reaching the tower to find the entrance to the church. Then continue south through the graveyard to the south-western corner, to follow a path along the south-east side of the playing fields in a slight gulley at the base of a bank underneath poplar trees. Some industrial premises lie ahead. On reaching them bear left and continue straight on, following the tarmac entrance road along the south side of the main factory and past the Sarasota office entrance. The Winchester to Newbury Road (A34) was built on a disused railway line and the embankment supporting it is ahead. On reaching the fencing at the base of the embankment, turn left following the base of the embankment on a path fenced on both sides for 100 metres where you will find a double set of tunnels. These take pedestrians under the south and northbound carriageways. On emerging on the other side turn left to follow the base of the northbound carriageway. On reaching one of the many channels comprising the route of the river Itchen through the water meadows turn right to head south-west towards Winchester along a path called Nuns Walk.

The river bears left away from the path and then another tributary is crossed by a footbridge next to a large pipeline. The path now follows the boundary between the water meadows on the left and open fields to the right towards Abbotts Barton. After passing along the south-east side of a large field the path rejoins the banks of the tributary, which is on the left. Continue along the south-east side of the second field, with another water channel only 50 metres further to the south-east. After passing along the south-east side of the third field, the path goes to the left of the first of the houses in Abbotts Barton. Then turn left over a concrete road bridge over the tributary and right again to continue to follow the stream along a gravel roadway.

After 500 metres the roadway turns right over the stream via a bridge. Do not cross this bridge but continue ahead on a gravel path on the south-east side of the stream. After 100 metres ignore the next road bridge and continue along the south-east side, this time on a tarmac pathway towards that part of Winchester called Hyde. Before reaching the older housing in Nuns Road, turn left along a specially constructed gravel path to the south of an athletics track to enter North Walls recreation ground open to the public under the management of Winchester City Council. The gravel path leads to a tarmac roadway.

Turn right along it to follow the north-west side of the recreation ground past the connection into Nuns Road. Follow the east bank of a stream on a wide tarmac pathway to reach the car park next to the Winchester City's River Park Leisure Centre. Before reaching that building turn left to continue to follow the stream with tennis courts on the left to cross over a large hump-backed ornamental footbridge over a waterway and turn right. After 100 metres following the waterway, cross another footbridge and then bear left to continue down Park Avenue with Winchester School of Art on the left until you reach the road called North Walls. Use the pedestrian crossing to continue straight on down Middle Brook Street and its continuation, Brook Street, to join High Street where you should turn left to reach the starting point in Broadway (see town centre map on page 64).

Historical Notes

Lord Eversley: Just before reaching the A33 on this walk you pass along the south side of the grounds of Abbots Worthy House to which Lord Eversley came in 1896 and stayed until his death in 1928 at the age of 97. He and his wife are buried in St Mary's churchyard at Kings Worthy and there is an urn on a enscribed pedestal in the south-east corner. He was Postmaster-General in Gladstone's government and introduced sixpenny telegrams, but his main preoccupation was access to commons and parks around London. He chaired the first meeting of the Commons Preservation Society in 1866, was author of a book entitled *Commons, Forests and Footpaths* published in 1894 and left £1,000 in his will to the Commons and Footpath Preservation Society. He has earned his place in the history of rambling.

St Mary's Church, Kings Worthy: This is an ancient place of worship. The present church is mainly from periods of reconstruction in 1849, 1864 and 1884 but the tower including the doorway and the font base are Late Norman and known rectors date from at least 1290. Its flint-faced façade seems to fit admirably into this Hampshire village. A guide is available inside by the Kings Worthy Local History Group.

Winnall Moors Nature Reserve: This walk passes close by the entrance to this nature reserve which is on the east side of the North Walls Recreation Ground. (See map on page 68). A footbridge takes you into an area of 100 acres of former water meadows and a specially constructed pathway over a mile in length takes you around its perimeter with an opportunity to take another path to a hide overlooking a pond in the centre. The numerous water channels enable visitors to see the wild fowl and the wildlife without much chance of interfering with their normal activities. The walk includes a long section along an unspoilt part of the river Itchen. Display boards indicate what you are likely to see on your visit. Further information can be obtained by sending a stamped, addressed envelope to the Hampshire and Isle of Wight Naturalists' Trust Ltd at its offices at 71, The Hundred, Romsey, Hampshire SO51 8BZ.

Winchester City Mill: This is a National Trust property which you pass at the start of this walk. Built in 1744 it has an impressive mill race and island garden and is leased to the Youth Hostel Association. It is open to visitors during the day in the tourist season. As a 58 bed hostel it is well located as an overnight stop for those wishing to split the Itchen Way into two parts. For membership details send an SAE to the YHA at Trevelyan House, 8 St Stephen's Hill, St Albans, Herts.

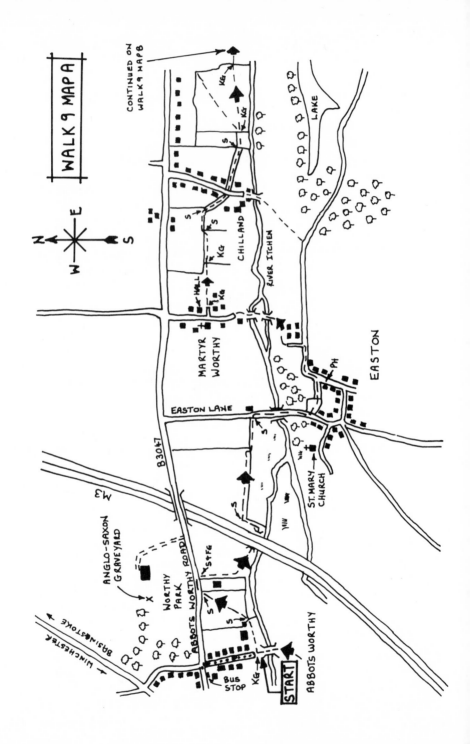

Abbots Worthy to Itchen Stoke

Introduction: The upper Itchen valley is a series of picturesque villages strung out along a watercourse that winds, often through numerous channels, through meadows and marshes against a backdrop of downs. The rich variety of the architecture and the quality of the housing is a pleasure to behold. This walk is one I frequently use to show visitors the real beauty of Hampshire, taking in one of the public houses en route. A good place for a lunch is the Chestnut Horse at Easton or the Plough Inn at Itchen Abbas. There are historic churches at Easton, Martyr Worthy, Itchen Abbas, Avington and Itchen Stoke. If Avington House is open, allow two hours for a walk around the grounds and the house. The walk finishes at Itchen Stoke, with a return journey by bus to Abbots Worthy.

Distance: Just under 5 miles (7.6 km) of very easy walking but could be muddy and flooded in parts in the winter months. Good walking boots are recommended.

Parking: This is a linear walk using the Winchester to Alresford bus route either to get to the start if you park in Itchen Stoke or to get back to Abbots Worthy or Kings Worthy if you park near the start. There is no recognised parking place at either end and parking is difficult in the narrow lanes so choose a spot where you will not inconvenience or obstruct local traffic.

Return: Use bus Service 214 operated by Alder Valley – for details telephone Winchester 52352, Alton 83787 or Guildford 575226/7; or the Service 908 operated by Classic Buses Limited of 2 Wales Street, Winchester. See the maps for the location of the bus stops.

Itchen Way – Abbots Worthy to Itchen Stoke: This eighth stage is the whole of Walk Nine once you have located the footbridge over the Itchen in Abbots Worthy. On reaching Itchen Stoke turn to Walk Twelve at page 96.

The Walk: The start is the bus stop in Abbots Worthy Road, Abbots Worthy near the junction with Mill Lane. Go down Mill Lane and just before you reach the end of the tarmac road and a three arched bridge over the river Itchen there is a metal kissing gate on the left which takes you into a small field to the right or south of some farm buildings. Pass to the right of the furthest farm building at the south-east corner of which there is a stile. Once in the field beyond, head to the north-east corner where there is a stile leading back out onto the road between Abbots Worthy and Alresford. Turn right along the road, with the grounds of Worthy Park to the north. To the west of the house there was discovered an Anglo-Saxon graveyard which yielded much information about the type, size and lifestyle of the early inhabitants of the valley. After 50 metres turn right over a stile next to a field gate and down the west and south sides of the field, heading towards the roar of the traffic on the M3. Take the pedestrian tunnel under the motorway and then a fenced path northwards along the east side of the motorway and over a stile into the field beyond. Follow the south side of this cropped field eastwards, with a pasture between you and the river Itchen to the south. Along this path you will see, to the south, the church of St Mary, Easton, dating from the middle of the 12th century. Buried here is Agatha Barlow who died in 1595 and whose five daughters all married bishops; her son was rector here. Two hundred metres before Easton Lane the path switches over into the aforementioned pastureland to follow the north side of the field eastwards to a stile onto the lane.

Turn right and follow the road towards Easton, crossing the various courses of the Itchen. Easton, a name coming from the Saxon referring to a 'ton' or village east of Winchester, is a pleasant village with a number of thatched properties and two public houses; it is worth a small detour. Immediately after passing the first group of cottages in the village, a footpath heads eastwards over a roadside stile. Head to the south-east corner of the field where there is another stile and continue east on a path between two fences to emerge out into the street at the eastern end of the village, quite fortuitously at the Chestnut Horse public house!

Take the road north and then east out of the village. Two hundred metres after turning east there is a gravel road heading north to some houses. Follow it and after 75 metres you leave the gravel track to go through a metal side gate into a field and then turn right. In 100 metres, after crossing a small ditch, turn left to follow the east side of the ditch to reach the village of Martyr Worthy via two footbridges over the Itchen.

On reaching the minor tarmaced road in the village, head north along it to pick up the public footpath heading east opposite the pedestrian entrance to the 12th century church. It starts as a gravel road running along the south side of the village hall. Pass through a kissing gate to enter the field beyond and continue due east across it. Ignore a field gate passing to the right of it to proceed to the eastern boundary to take a kissing gate into the field to the east and not an older version leading into the field to the north. Continue east on the north side of a field and cross over a stile into the field beyond and then continue east, this time on the south side of a field. Cross a stile in the south-east corner and then there is a clear change of direction to the south-east. The path is now between fences and ends by emerging onto a road in the village of Chilland.

Cross the road and bear left to pick up a footpath heading east towards Itchen Abbas. After an initial unsightly section between fences you cross a stile and burst out into fields with the river Itchen to the south. There is a short fenced section adjacent to the river and then, after going through a kissing gate, there is a larger field ahead. Two paths leave this point, one north-east, the other east. Follow the latter, gradually attaining higher ground by moving slightly away from the river. Pass through another kissing gate where there is a fine view down onto the river and the grounds of Avington Park beyond.

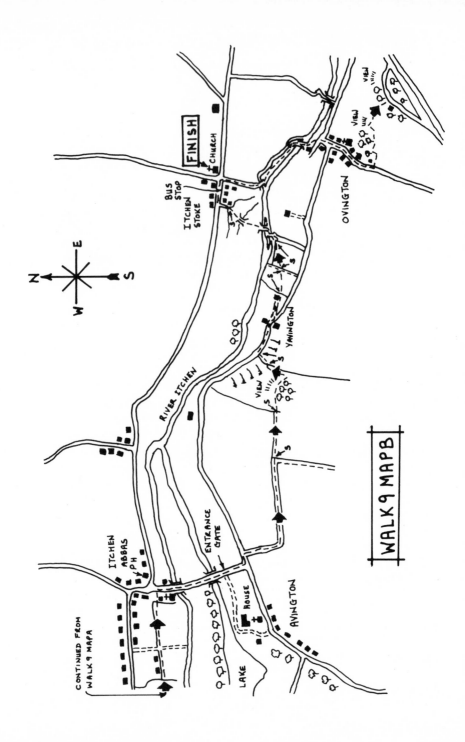

After reaching the north-east corner of the next field, you reach two kissing gates in quick succession either side of a drive leading down to the river. The path eastwards to Itchen Abbas is now fenced on both sides.

Once out onto the road, turn left for The Plough Inn in 30 metres or, to continue the walk, turn right along the road past the church of St John the Baptist. Although an ancient Christian site the current building dates from 1863 when the old one was demolished. On approaching the church on the left there is an old yew tree where there is the grave of John Hughes, a gypsy who was the last man to be hanged for horse stealing. He stole the horse of the Rev Robert Wright who arranged for the body to be buried here.

Heading south, the road crosses twin road bridges over the Itchen and then crosses the waters feeding Avington Lake and past the entrance to Avington Park (see Historical Notes). At the first bend in the road there is a junction; take the road to the east before turning right in 20 metres to continue south-east uphill along a farm road, initially concreted. It then turns to gravel and 300 metres from the public road it turns left to head eastwards. After initially being level the roadway drops downhill into a gulley to turn sharp right and head south, but at this point head east into a field via a stile to follow its north side. The path then turns south-east and goes along the north side of an isolated plantation of trees where a panoramic view northwards opens up. You can see the village of Itchen Stoke with Alresford beyond. After reaching the eastern boundary of the field, follow it downhill to the north-east and in the north-eastern corner there is a stile leading the walker over into the field to the east. Drop down to cross over the stile in the north-west corner onto the road between Avington and Ovington.

Follow the road south-east past Yavington Farm Cottage on the left and the farm buildings opposite, to fork left down the access way leading to Yavington Mead. Respecting the occupiers' privacy, pass immediately to the right (south) of this splendid house, past the back door and via a stile into the field beyond. Cross the field eastward to a double set of stiles where there used to be a double fence line but now there is just one.

Continue east in the following field along the northern side to the north-eastern end of the field where there is a stile leading out onto a footpath along a green lane.

Once out into the green lane, turn left along the narrow track between hedgerows and after 100 metres the first of two footbridges is reached over the river Itchen. After another 25 metres the second much larger footbridge takes one over the main river. There is a small gate at the northern end of the bridge leading out into the field beyond. Follow a track in the grass northwards. Immediately on the right is a sluice in the water meadow system. The path is heading to the main road between Itchen Abbas and Alresford on the north side of the valley. Two hundred metres from the footbridge, bear right to cross an agricultural road bridge over a water channel and then head towards a field gate visible to the left of some picturesque dwellings ahead. This is the village of Itchen Stoke which dates from the 17th and 18th centuries but there is a lost medieval village which existed in AD 960 and was recorded in the Domesday Book. There is a stile to the left of the field gate which takes you into a 100 metre long track to the main road. Turn right along the main road, taking care as there is no footway. It is 350 metres to the centre of the village where there is a crossroads dominated by the church of St Mary on the south-west corner of which is the wooden bus stop and a telephone box.

Historical Notes

Avington House: South of Itchen Abbas a large part of the valley floor provides a lake and the grounds for this fine house which is open to the public (1989) between May and September on Saturdays, Sundays and Bank Holidays between 2.30pm and 5.30pm for a charge of £1.50. There is an Orangery Tea Bar where visitors can take refreshment in a tranquil setting. If the house is open it will be advertised on the wrought iron entrance gates dating from 1700 passed on this walk. Roman remains have been found at the site, and it is known that Avington has existed as a settlement since at least AD 961 when Edgar, the King of the Angles, transferred the house and the Manses of Afintun to the Cathedral of Winchester. In 1545 it was surrendered to Henry VIII and a year later he sold it to Edmund Clerke. The history of the families who have owned it since is described in a good guide book available at the house when it is open. On the south side of the park is a church and like most religious sites in this valley there has been a church here for 1,000 years. The Saxon church was demolished in the 18th century but the Georgian replacement is a small, attractive one. Above the central elevation of the house are three lead statues representing the goddesses Minerva, Juno and Ceres, weighing over three tons each. The main features of the southern elevation are two large conservatories dating from about 1850.

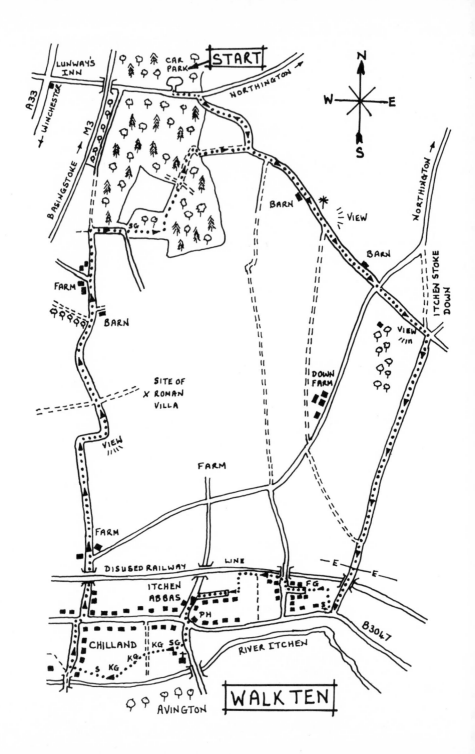

START

LUNWAY'S INN

CAR PARK

A33

← WINCHESTER

BASINGSTOKE

M3

NORTHINGTON →

N
W · E
S

NORTHINGTON

BARN

VIEW

BARN

ITCHEN STOKE DOWN

SG

FARM

BARN

VIEW

SITE OF ROMAN VILLA

DOWN FARM

FARM

VIEW

FARM

FARM

DISUSED RAILWAY LINE

E — E — E

ITCHEN ABBAS

FG

PH

CHILLAND

KG SG

KG

S KG

RIVER ITCHEN

B3047

AVINGTON

WALK TEN

Itchen Wood to Chilland

Introduction: North of the upper river Itchen is a large area of sparsely populated, rolling downland with many ancient by-ways and bridleroads from which extensive views are available. This area in pre-Roman times would have been covered with woodland, but now only a few well managed woods remain and most of the area is prime farmland full of wildlife. From a car park in Micheldever Wood the walk follows an ancient unsurfaced bridleroad running all the way to Alresford. The walk leaves this route on the hills above Abbotstone to follow another unsurfaced track over the disused Winchester to Alresford railway line to Itchen Abbas to follow the river Itchen past the church of St John the Baptist with views across the field to Avington House. From the pretty village of Chilland it is back across the downs and through Itchen Wood to complete this circular route.

Distance: 7½ miles (12 km) with many ups and downs although easy underfoot. The only problem is likely to come in fog or snow. Allow 2½ to 3½ hours, depending on the pace.

Parking: The start of the walk is a Forestry Commission managed car park, open subject to bylaws. It is on a minor road which leaves the A33 between Winchester and Basingstoke eastward at a point on a section of dual carriageway 3 miles north of Kings Worthy, marked by the Lunway's Inn on the south-east corner of the junction. The road is signposted to The Candovers and Northington. Going eastward the road goes under the M3 and then Micheldever Wood is to the north and Itchen Wood is to the south. The car park is 500 metres from the M3 on the left.

Bus Services: Mervyn's Coaches of 3 Chapel Close, Dummer, Basingstoke, RG25 2AB, telephone Dummer (025675) 719, operate Services 95, 96 and 96a from Winchester and Basingstoke to Lunway's Inn where there would be just over a mile to walk to the start and the same back; or the Alder Valley service (see Walk Nine) could be used to start the walk either at Chilland or Itchen Abbas.

Itchen Way: Although this walk uses part of the Itchen Way in reverse, long distance walkers should turn to Walk Twelve and page 96 to continue this walk.

The Walk: Leave the car park by returning to the road and turning left along it, eastward for 200 metres. On the right, just before the end of the woodland take an unsurfaced byway going off to the right heading south-east. Ignore an entrance into Itchen Wood immediately on the right and continue along the edge of the wood following the track between fences as it passes between two fields. It then begins a climb uphill in a tunnel of vegetation. Eventually the top of the hill is reached and the byway descends downhill, turning more to the right to go southwards. At the bottom of the hill there is a track off to the right towards Itchen Wood which is the return route for this walk. Here turn left to go south-eastwards steadily uphill on the continuation of the byway. In 200 metres there is a bridleway off to the right but continue straight on along a well established chalk roadway. Still climbing after ¼ mile you pass a modern hay barn on the right and the track becomes tarmaced. Continue south-east towards a wind pump on the skyline 500 metres ahead at one of the highest points in the area.

Once over the ridge a magnificent view southward across the valley of the Itchen opens up. Do not get too absorbed in the scene ahead because almost immediately it is necessary to fork left along a chalk road, leaving the tarmac road to bear off down right, south-west towards Itchen Down Farm. Ahead you can see the byway heading downhill and then up the other side towards Alresford visible in the distance. Cheesefoot Head Hill is visible to the south-west. After passing another modern hay barn on the left, the byway reaches the valley bottom and the road between Itchen Abbas and Northington. Cross over the road and follow the continuation of the byway uphill out of the valley. The byway is between barbed wire fences and, as you begin to descend over the other side of the ridge, older hedges come in view marking the junction of no less than five rights-of-way. The route for this walk is to the right, heading south-west along the bottom of a shallow valley. This area is known as Itchen Stoke Down and the bridleway is leading towards Itchen Abbas down in the valley full of trees ahead.

After ¾ mile of gradual descent between hedges, the track begins to go uphill. As it levels out again there is a bridleway to the right or north-west which is the continuation of the tarmaced track which you would have left near the wind pump. Continue south-west, however, in the same direction as before and begin the descent to the main road along the north side of the Itchen valley. On the way you pass under some electricity power lines and then across a bridge over a disused railway line between Kings Worthy and Alresford.

On reaching the main road turn right and in 10 metres on the right, to the right of a field gate, is a stile leading into a field to the right of a fence line going northwards. To the west is a large private house. Continue up the west side of the field under a substantial line of beech trees along a footpath. The field is L-shaped and on reaching the inside corner of the 'L' turn left to go west under yet more trees, around a tank to leave the field via a field gate into an urban cul-de-sac called Baring Close. Follow it to Rectory Lane, turn right here and go uphill towards the disused railway line again to take a footpath on the left immediately before the bridge over the former cutting. The path follows the lineside hedge. After leaving the houses behind there is an open field to the south sloping down to the main road. Just beyond its western boundary there is a footpath down to that road but continue to follow the lineside fence along the north side of the next field along a fenced pathway under trees. After another 200 metres turn left, following the pathway southwards for 50 metres and then turn right continuing downhill westward towards Itchen Abbas. After 100 metres you join a tarmaced roadway at an entrance to a private house called Little Hayes. Continue westward on the roadway past the school until you reach Northington Road. Turn left here and in 100 metres the B3047 is reached at the crossroads in the centre of the village where there is a telephone box and a bus stop. Bear left along the main road where you will find The Plough Inn.

Turn right just before the inn along the road to Avington and ahead on the right is the gateway entrance to the church of St John the Baptist. To the right of the gateway a footpath commences up a gravel driveway and, on reaching the second house, continues up a grass track to a field gate to the right of which is a side gate marking the start of a path fenced on both sides heading west towards Chilland. The church and house at Avington can be briefly seen along this path in the trees to the south. Follow the path along the back of the large houses fronting the B3047 until it crosses a driveway and avenue of trees leading down to the river Itchen below. Cross over the drive and go through the kissing gate located between two field gates into the field next to the Itchen. At the north-western corner of the field pass through another kissing gate and continue westward along the northern boundary of the next field, heading for the western boundary where there is a kissing gate next to the river. Beyond it there is a short section of path along the riverside fenced from the field to the north. It ends at a stile; cross over it and along an unattractive fenced section of path until you reach a tarmaced road in Chilland.

Turn right along the road and follow it uphill towards the B3047 again. Turn right and almost immediately left up a minor road running north. It passes under a short tunnel under the disused railway, then ignore the roadway to the right and continue straight on following the road past farm buildings on the right and Chillandham Cottages up on the left. It is uphill all the way for just under ½ mile where the tarmac road turns right and 200 metres later left to continue northwards. Behind is the valley of the Itchen filled with the trees that form the setting to Avington Park House.

After another 300 metres the crest of the ridge is reached where there is a concrete surfaced roadway running down west to Bridget's Farm and an unsurfaced roadway running east to where the site of a Roman villa has been found. Continue to follow the tarmac road north, which is level now. It then begins to descend with views of Itchen Wood ahead to where this walk will lead. The road bears right and just after that there is a farm track off to the left along the north side of a tree shelter belt. Just beyond that a track on the right leads to a modern hay barn. Continue to follow the road towards Chillandham Farm which is visible ahead on the left-hand side of the road. The tarmac road turns left into the farm, but at this point continue straight ahead uphill, following a chalk road passing to the right or east of the farmhouse. A hundred metres beyond it there is a crossroads of rights-of-way and here turn right along another chalk road passing along the southern end of Itchen Wood. After 300 metres the chalk road turns right. There is also a track on the left into a field entirely surrounded by woodland. Continue straight on, however, at this point in the same direction through a side gate next to a field gate to enter an area of wood called the Scrubbs. The track ahead is a bridleway and through the woods to the south a field is visible. After 300 metres, just as you come up level with the north-east corner of that field, the path bends through 90 degrees to head northwards with Courtney's Copse on the right. After 200 metres the eastern side of the field surrounded by woods is reached.

Continue in the woodland following the eastern side of that pasture to its north-eastern corner. At that corner there is a crossroads of tracks; continue straight on in the same direction into Itchen Wood. After 300 metres a field gate with a side gate next to it is reached; continue straight on to emerge on the eastern edge of the wood. Follow the track as it bends right and then left along the south side of the field heading east. At the south-east corner you rejoin the outward route. Turn left to follow the old byway in a tunnel of vegetation on the east side of the aforementioned field. Initially it is a climb, but after bending north-westward it begins to descend to join the road between the A33 and Northington. Turn left along the road and the car park is 200 metres on the right.

Historical Notes

Plough Inn: In the former inn on this site Charles Kingsley, the famous 19th century author, wrote part of *The Water Babies*.

Disused Railway Line: Although now being filled in to reclaim it to farmland on the sections visited on this walk, this was the line which ran from the main Bournemouth to Waterloo line west of Kings Worthy to Alton. From Alresford via Ropley and Four Marks to Alton the line has been preserved as a steam railway, the famous Watercress Line. For a timetable and information on their special events write to the Mid-Hants Railway plc, Alresford Station, Alresford SO24 9JG, or telephone (0962) 734200 or 733810. Try parking at Alton, getting a return to Alresford and doing Walk Eleven.

Roman Villas: All over Hampshire there are sites of Roman villas, centres of prosperous farming estates which over more than 300 years of Roman occupation were enhanced with mosaic floors, painted walls, pottery and glass. The term 'villa' was used to denote not just a house but all the farm and outbuildings. It would include separate rooms for eating, sleeping, and entertaining, some with under-floor heating, kitchens and very hot bath houses. Most worthwhile artefacts have been taken to local museums and there is rarely anything visible on site. The exceptions like the palace at Fishbourne near Chichester in Sussex, the villas at Brading on the Isle of Wight and Rockbourne near Fordingbridge could give an indication of the good living to be had in those days in the valley of the Itchen.

Alresford and Itchen Stoke Down

Introduction: New Alresford has all the ingredients necessary to entertain the tourist for a day but to the inhabitants it is the setting in attractive downland with the splendours of the valleys of the rivers Arle and Candover which are equally as important. This circular walk shows these features at their best. From Broad Street the walk goes down to the river Arle and the historic Fulling Mill before following a valley with watercress beds leading to Old Alresford. Then it is over the downs on green lanes to the site of the medieval village of Abbotstone and the valley of the Candover Stream. From Itchen Stoke Down there are enjoyable views over the Candover which is crossed again below Fob Down as the walk leads back along the lakes and waterways of the river Arle to New Alresford.

Distance: 5½ miles (8.8 km) with some climbing. Can be muddy in wet weather but going generally easy.

How to get there: By train from the London area to Alton by British Rail and then by the Mid-Hants Railway to Alresford. By bus from Winchester using Service 214 and 215 (Alder Valley) or Service 67 (Hampshire Bus); from Alton Services 214 or 215; from Petersfield by Service 67; and from Basingstoke by Service 309 operated by Oakley Coaches.

Parking: If Alresford has a problem it is parking in the tourist season. There are a number of well signposted locations but patience will be required to find a spot. The main blessing is that the southern by-pass has now eradicated most of the through traffic.

Itchen Way: This walk is included because the Candover Stream and the river Arle contribute greatly to the flows in the upper river Itchen, but none of the route is on the Itchen Way so long distance walkers should continue by turning to Walk Twelve on page 96.

The Walk: The start of this walk is in a wide tree-lined avenue called Broad Street in the centre of New Alresford north of the B3047. On the west side is Laurence Oxley's book-shop. Head north from here and on the left is the house where Mary Russell Mitford was born in 1787. From here cross over to the east side and on the right where the road narrows down to become The Soke is the old fire station. Ahead is The Globe public house. Just before it on the left is a footpath along a narrow access road to some houses at the end of which turn left along a path leading to a footbridge over a fast flowing water chute. Just beyond you join Mill Hill road with the converted Town Mill on the right. Turn left here for 20 metres and then right down Ladywell Lane which is a narrow tarmaced road; follow the narrow raised footway on the left until it rejoins the lane. The road ends at the entrance at Arle House where a gravel surfaced footpath continues between fences. After 200 metres there is an area of open space dedicated to The Fallen of both World Wars. Continue straight on here over a water sluice and along the south side of the river Arle towards the 13th century Fulling Mill, a white timber-framed building with a thatched roof.

After passing to the left of the mill, turn right over the river directly in front of the mill to leave it going north-east along the gravel roadway providing vehicular access to the mill. In 100 metres you meet a road with a view towards the church of St Mary the Virgin at Old Alresford ahead. Turn left along the road across the valley filled with watercress beds and, just as the road begins to rise, take a gravel surfaced roadway on the right which leads to and passes to the right of a pair of cottages and then a house. Just beyond the house is a stile leading into the field to the north. Continue along the eastern boundary towards Old Alresford and, at the north-east corner on the approach to Manor Farm, drop down right to join a farm road going north, passing between the old farmhouse to the right and a newer dwelling on the left. Then pass to the right of an L-shaped thatched barn and then a set of farm buildings, and 50 metres beyond, where the roadway bends down right, turn left uphill along an unsurfaced byway in a gulley between hedges. It is a steady climb for ¼ mile to the top of the ridge where there is another grassy byway down to the left. At this point continue straight on, heading for Abbotstone, and the track bends first slightly right then left rising again, past a grassy farm track on the right. The track then levels out and begins to gradually descend with good views in a southerly arc. Fobdown Farm comes into view down to the left. The main vehicular traffic takes a byway to the left down to the farm but continue straight on at this junction along a grassy byway between hedges. After ⅓ mile there is a distinctly sharp left-hand bend in the byway where it changes direction from north-west to west. Now on the left is the site of a medieval village recognizable by the humps and bumps in the fields. Three hundred metres from that left-hand bend you join the tarmaced road from Old Alresford to Abbotstone, the latter consisting now of only the few cottages and a large farm on the river Candover below.

Follow the road downhill, ignoring the tarmaced road on the right towards Abbotstone Farm which is the northward route of the Wayfarers Walk which is now joined for the rest of the route back to Alresford. Continue across the valley floor, crossing the Candover, and at the road junction near a pair of attractive thatched cottages continue straight on up an unsurfaced byway incorrectly signposted as a 'no through road'. It is a steady climb for ½ mile along this byway to get to the top of Itchen Stoke Down where there is a crossroads of five rights-of-way, all of them grass-covered tracks. Turn left following the Wayfarers Walk south-eastward along the top of the ridge. After ⅓ mile go straight across the tarmaced road between

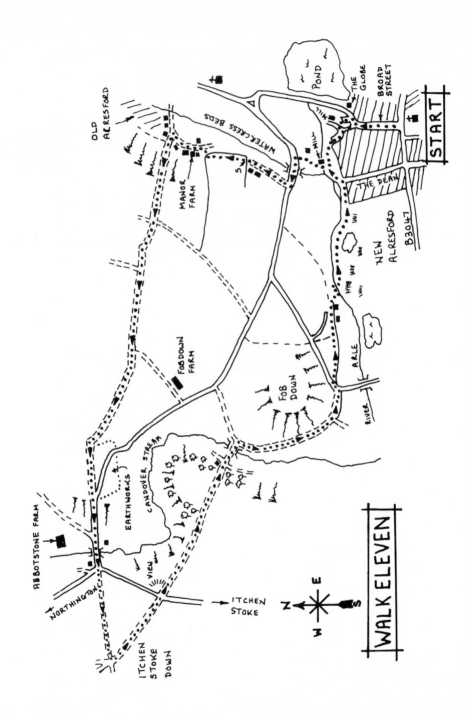

START

BROAD STREET

THE GLOBE

MILL POND

MILL

THE DEAN

NEW ALRESFORD

B3047

WATERCRESS BEDS

OLD ALRESFORD

MANOR FARM

FOB DOWN FARM

FOB DOWN

ALRE

RIVER

EARTHWORKS

CANDOVER STREAM

ABBOTSTONE FARM

NORTHINGTON

VIEW

ITCHEN STOKE

ITCHEN STOKE DOWN

N E S W

WALK ELEVEN

Itchen Stoke and Abbotstone, although it is worth pausing to catch the view eastward across the valley of the Candover.

The leafy, grassy lane now begins a gradual descent but it is over ½ mile before you descend to the valley of the Candover and reach the valley floor and a crossroads of tracks near a flint-faced cottage. Continue straight on along the track across the valley floor, with yet more watercress beds and once over the Candover turn right at a T-junction. Heading south along this byway, following the river valley, Fob Down makes its presence felt on the left after ¼ mile as you begin to ascend, working around the south-west slopes of the hill. The byway levels out and then the houses in New Alresford come into view. Ignore a track going down to the right and continue to follow the byway as it bends left until reaching a sharp bend in the tarmac road between the western end of New Alresford and Old Alresford.

Turn left and in 50 metres bear off the road to the right on a track following a tree-lined hedge. The tarmac road continues to rise up the slopes of Fob Down but the track is virtually level and through the trees on the right you can see some lakes along the course of the river Arle. After 300 metres there is a footpath left up to the road but continue in the same direction. Almost immediately you pass between a house on the right and an entrance road on the left and enter a section of the path which is fenced on both sides. After passing a second house on the right there is a stile on the left. A right-of-way continues north-eastward at this point but drop down right following the main track to cross over a footbridge over an aqueduct next to the Arle. Continue east between the two watercourses; after 50 metres turn right across the river next to a small brick building to continue eastward along the south side of the river with the odd pond and marshy terrain to the right. A footbridge over a sluice is crossed in 100 metres and then a much larger lake is passed on the right. There are wildfowl everywhere here, and Old Alresford church and the watercress beds seen earlier are visible to the north-east. Next there is an island in the river and the path turns right to cross over to the south side of a ditch and continues to follow the river on slightly higher ground.

After passing a gravestone on the right you finally reach the houses in New Alresford on the right and the path exits onto the end of a road called The Dean leading uphill to the centre of New Alresford.

It is recommended that you turn left here to follow the banks of the Arle past the eastern end of the island and some seats, then cross a footbridge over a sluice. The river bends to the right, turning east to the Fulling Mill where you continue straight on to follow the route taken on the outward journey. At the eastern end of Ladywell Lane you can turn right to get back up hill to Broad Street where the walk began.

Historical Notes

Mary Russell Mitford: Born at Mitford House, 27 Broad Street, Alresford on 16th December 1787 and later a resident of 6 East Street, this novelist and dramatist was famous for her articles and sketches of country life and character. In the book *Our Village* which is about Three Mile Cross she gave a good insight into early 19th century life. She died at Swallowfield, near Reading on 10th January 1855.

Old Alresford Pond: The rear garden of The Globe pub backs onto this pond. It is also visible from the end of the little access road, Pond View, next to The Globe. It was constructed as a reservoir of 200 acres by Godfrey de Lucy who was enthroned as Bishop of Winchester in 1189. The pond is much reduced in size now but the original intention was to expand New Alresford as a wool centre. He developed the idea of constructing the Great Weir to assist the control of navigation up the Itchen from Southampton by flat bottomed boats. He laid out the town, the pattern of which is still intact, and the supply of water was used to run mills. Broad Street was the market place.

Itchen Stoke to Ovington

Introduction: This short circular walk incorporates some excellent views over the downs and valleys on both sides of the Itchen as well as a pretty walk along river banks and over interesting footbridges. The start is high up above Ovington which is the first village to be visited after passing Ovington House and the church of St Peter. Then going west past Lovington House and turning down a pretty path to the double footbridges over the Itchen leading to Itchen Stoke, the route crosses disused water meadows. The church of St Mary in Itchen Stoke is where Water Lane is taken on the return route to one of the prettiest sections of the Itchen Way, leading across another footbridge to the Bush Inn at Ovington before the climb back up to the Alresford Road.

Distance: Just under 3 miles (4.5 km). Some of the walk is on roads where care is needed because of the danger of approaching vehicles. The end of the walk is the ascent up from Ovington and the paths in the river valley could be flooded in really wet weather.

Parking: The start is on a layby with public toilets on the Alresford Road, the A31 from Winchester to Alton, ½ mile south-west of the roundabout at the western end of the Alresford bypass. It is a section of the old road.

Bus Services: Hampshire Bus Service 67 goes past the start on its way between Winchester and Petersfield via Alresford. Alternatively it is possible to start at Itchen Stoke using the services mentioned in Walk Nine.

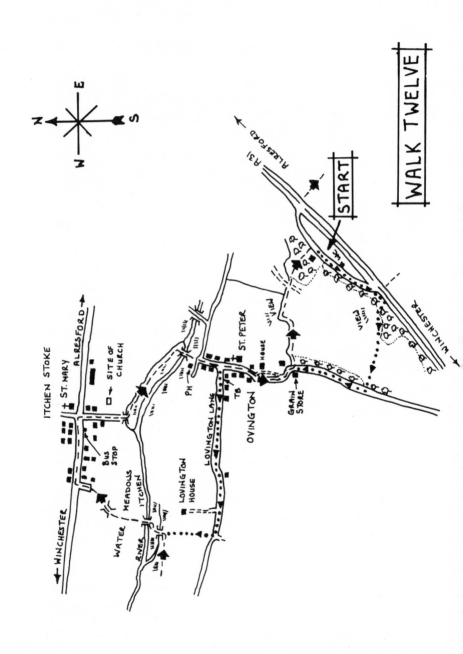

WALK TWELVE

Itchen Way – Itchen Stoke to Ovington: This ninth stage starts half way through Walk Twelve at the church of St Mary, Itchen Stoke (page 96) and follows the remainder of the walk to a layby on part of the old Alresford Road above Ovington from where long distance walkers should turn to Walk Thirteen which starts at this layby.

The Walk: At the south-western end of the layby where vehicles enter it from the dual carriageway, go along the north side of the main road for 100 metres to the signposted start of a footpath. Do not follow the obvious track running parallel with the road which is the remains of the old road, but turn immediately into the plantation, across some earth banks to reach the highest side of the field beyond. Below in the valley bottom is a road running north to Ovington. The only navigational clue is the section of wood that juts out into the field (see map opposite). Follow the edge of the wood downhill and then head across the field to the western boundary aiming for the point where the roadside plantation coming from the north narrows down to a line of roadside trees. Just to the south of this point there is a set of steps and footpath sign indicating the point where you descend to the road. Take care because this point is on a bend.

Turn right along the road, heading north towards Ovington. In 300 metres the road passes to the right of Park Farm grain store and then bears left at the southern entrance to Ovington House, the perimeter wall of which is followed by the road. After a double bend at the northern entrance to the house the village of Ovington is entered with the church of St Peter on the right. At the road junction just beyond, turn left into Lovington Lane and past a telephone box on the left. Quickly the village is left behind and the lane descends for ¼ mile into a shallow valley and up the other side. Around a double bend you pass Lovington Cottages on the left and then the entrance to Lovington House, which is visible down on the right. Then the lane begins to descend again into another shallow valley. At the bottom there is a bridleway on the left up to Hampage Wood but take the footpath on the right which leads downhill in a gulley towards the river Itchen.

After crossing the first of two footbridges over the river Itchen bear to the right and cross the second one over the much larger watercourse. There is a small gate at the northern end of the bridge leading out into the field beyond. Follow a track in the grass northwards. Immediately on the right is a sluice in the disused water meadow system. The path is heading to the main road between Itchen Abbas and Alresford on the north side of the valley. Two hundred metres from the footbridge bear right to cross an agricultural road bridge over a water channel and then head towards a field gate visible to the left of some dwellings ahead. On approaching the gate it will be seen that there is a stile to the left of it leading into a 100 metre long track to the main road.

Turn right along the main road, taking care as there is no footway. It is 350 metres to the centre of the village where there is a crossroads dominated by the church of St Mary, on the south-west corner of which is the wooden bus stop and a telephone box.

This is the point where **The Itchen Way** continues from the end of Walk Nine. Turn right down Water Lane, a narrow tarmaced road heading south to the river Itchen. Just after passing the last house called 'The Shallows', if you look through the hedge on the left you can see a fenced and wooded enclosure in the middle of the field which is the site of the original church and graveyard. The road ends at a footbridge; cross over it and turn left to follow a footpath south-east between the main river on the right and a narrow offshoot on the left heading towards Ovington. After 500 metres a large footbridge takes the walker over the main river to the south bank and into the village. On the right on reaching the road is The Bush Inn. From the end of the footpath go south uphill through the village of Ovington, past Lovington Lane on the right with its telephone box and then past the church of St Peter on the left. The road bears right at the northern entrance to Ovington House and follows the western boundary of the enclosed grounds which are hidden from view behind a flint wall. Lovely views are obtained of a valley to the right. When the flint wall ends at the southern entrance to the house a footpath leaves the road on the left.

The footpath sign points the way through a shelter belt of trees adjacent to the road and then you are out into an open field with a pleasant cottage to the left. Bear left following the irregular northern perimeter of the field with the garden associated with the cottage and then a wood to the north. As you near the north-eastern corner of the field you leave the woods behind and there is a magnificent view down over Ovington and the marshlands of the river Itchen. Near the north-eastern corner there is a track which links this field with that to the north-east. Ignore this and go right to the very north-east corner of the field and you will find a track leaving the field into the wood ahead which, after passing 50 metres to the left of a small lodge, emerges onto the old Alresford road which now forms a layby off the main dual carriageway. This was the point where you started.

Historical Notes

Itchen Stoke and Ovington: These villages, although modest in size and with few really old buildings, have existed since Anglo-Saxon times when they are recorded as having been transferred in the 10th century by King Edgar to the Bishop of Winchester. Ovington derives from Ofinetune, Saxon for 'the place above'. They are referred to in the Domesday Book commissioned by William the Conqueror in 1085. The first recorded church at Itchen Stoke was in 1270 and at Ovington in 1285, both of which have now been demolished.

In 1327 there were 24 households in Itchen Stoke paying taxes so the population must have been around 100 or even more. The original church was in Water Lane as mentioned above. It was described in John Duthy's famous book on the Itchen called *Sketches of Hampshire*. The church of St Mary the Virgin was built in 1866 and the architect was Henry Conybeare, brother of the then vicar, the Rev Charles Ranken

Conybeare, and his design is based on that of La Saint Chapelle in Paris. It is now in the care of the Redundant Churches Fund.

1866 also saw the construction of a new church of St Peter at Ovington. The site of the Norman church is to the north of the present building but only the arch of the entrance now remains in the graveyard.

Bush Inn: The name is a relic from the days when the population was largely illiterate and licencing laws did not curb the production and sale of beer. A bunch of twigs (like that shown on the pub sign) hanging above the door of a house would indicate that there was ale for sale.

WALK THIRTEEN

Tichborne

Introduction: Once above the confluence with the Arle and the Candover the river Itchen is reduced to a stream in a narrower valley but with the same attractive undulating countryside on either side. This circular walk takes a route around the village of Tichborne and its surrounding hills. Starting on the A31 high above Ovington and New Alresford there is initially a pretty descent to the Itchen near Vernal Farm. Then using paths to the edge of Alresford and back through the parkland near Tichborne House there follow extensive views of the Itchen Valley stretching south to Cheriton Mill. The return route is past Sevington Farm and the village of Tichborne including a visit to the lofty and interesting St Andrew's church. Before going back up to the A31 through downland and woodland you could enjoy the hospitality of the Tichborne Arms.

Distance: A walk of just over 4 miles (6.7 km). The walking is pleasant with a steady climb back out of Tichborne. The main problem could be wet grass or crops when waterproof boots will be required.

Parking: The start is on a layby with public toilets on the Alresford Road, the A31 from Winchester to Alton, ½ mile south-west of the roundabout at the western end of the Alresford Bypass. It is a section of the old road.

Bus Services: Hampshire Bus Service 67 goes past the start on its way between Winchester and Petersfield via Alresford.

Itchen Way – Ovington to Tichborne: This tenth stage starts with this walk from the old Alresford Road layby on the A31 reached at the end of Walk Twelve and continues following Walk Thirteen until Cheriton Mill south of Tichborne is reached. It continues after that at a point two thirds of the way through Walk Fourteen.

The Walk: To start this walk and to continue the Itchen Way head north-eastwards along the layby, following the old road until reaching the new Alresford Road which is a busy dual carriageway. Again there are good views north over the country-side beyond the Itchen. Cross over both lanes of the dual carriageway taking care because vehicles approach at high speed. Take a track opposite leading to a field gate and into the field on the south side of the road. Continue south-eastwards along the south-west side of the field with Trodds Copse to your right on the other side of the hedge. The copse was named after a Tichborne family. To the east can be seen New Alresford and to the east and south-east is the valley of the river Itchen to be explored on this walk. It is a flat walk to the south-western corner of the field where there is a stile into the field beyond. Once over the stile, turn immediately left to commence the descent to the Itchen following the north side of the field. At the north-eastern corner of the field go left through a gap in the hedge into the field to the north and continue east towards the road between Alresford and Tichborne. On the way down the river Itchen can be seen meandering through the valley to the north-east and under the Alresford Bypass.

On reaching the road cross over to follow a minor road leading to Vernal Farm which is a bridleway. Cross over the Itchen and straight on uphill to the right of the farm buildings and the house beyond which the track becomes a grassy bridleway between fences heading towards the Alresford Bypass. On reaching the edge of the bypass bear right, following a track between post and rail fencing directly above the bypass which is in a cutting. After 150 metres turn right over a stile into a triangular section of tree planting and over another stile into a field and along its south-eastern boundary, heading south-west towards Tichborne Park. After 200 metres go left over a stile and continue south-westwards along the side of another triangular plantation, over another stile, this time heading south-westward along the north-west side of a triangular shaped field. In the south-western corner of the field cross over a stile next to a vehicular entrance to the field and continue almost in the same direction to join a more substantial roadway coming from the north-west.

Follow this farm road heading south-south-west with fields to the left and the river Itchen to the right. This farm road is leading in the direction of Tichborne House, and Tichborne village can be seen across the valley; above and to the left is the field known as the Crawls (see Historical Notes). After 400 metres along the farm road a tarmac road is reached. Continue straight on along it towards the entrance gates to Tichborne House, 100 metres ahead. To the left of the gates is a stile; cross over it into a field to the east of Tichborne House and continue along its western boundary. The tennis courts and grounds associated with the house are on the opposite side of the hedge and to the east is a cricket pitch and pavilion. In the south-west corner of the field, cross over the stile, go across a narrow shelter plantation and over another stile next to a field gate. The river Itchen is off to the right, wending its way up the valley past Sevington Farm to the source south of Cheriton. Continue on in the same direction across the cropped field ahead to a stile in the south-eastern boundary fence. Cross the stile and in the field to the south-east it is necessary to bear further to the left, aiming for the second from the right of the high voltage electricity pylons in the distance to the south-east. The river Itchen is also bending around east with you and there is a view up the marshy valley bottom towards Cheriton. Near the south-eastern corner of the field the footpath leads out onto the New Alresford to Cheriton road some 50 metres to the left of a brick built cottage. There is a stile and a crude field entrance at this point.

Once onto the road turn right, and immediately after the cottage turn right along the road signposted to Tichborne. Having crossed over the river Itchen, Cheriton Mill lies to the

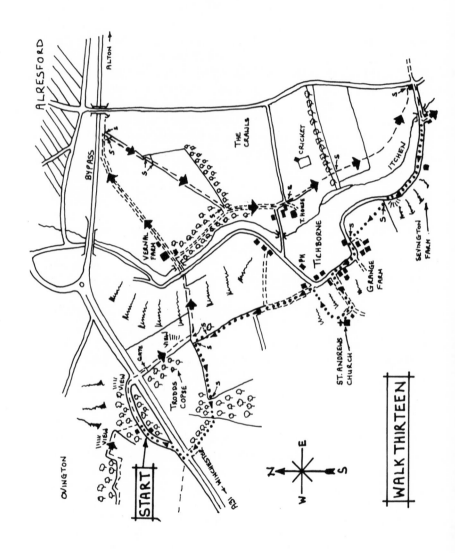

ALRESFORD

ALTON →

BYPASS

THE CRAWLS

CRICKET

ITCHEN

T. HOUSE

VERNAL FARM

PK

TICHBORNE

SEVINGTON FARM

GRANGE FARM

ST. ANDREWS CHURCH

TRODDS COPSE

VIEW

VIEW

GATE

OVINGTON

START

A31 WINCHESTER →

A31 → WINCHESTER

N
E
W
S

WALK THIRTEEN

left of the road. Those following the through route on **The Itchen Way** should turn left towards Cheriton to go up between the mill and the farm buildings.

To continue this circular walk follow the road towards Tichborne. Sevington Farm is on the left after 400 metres. The house dates from the 17th and 18th centuries but there has been a manor house for the Bishop of Winchester's Tichborne and Cheriton estates here from medieval times until 19th century. Just beyond is a collection of modern farm buildings at a point where the road bends right north-westward. After another 300 metres the road is running along the base of an escarpment to the left and by the sign announcing the arrival in Tichborne is the vehicular entrance into a small quarry. Just 5 metres beyond the entrance is a track leading up under a large beech tree to a stile leading into the field to the north-west. Ahead are the modern farm buildings associated with Grange Farm and just to the right is a white pair of semi-detached cottages. Head across the field north-westward to these cottages and, after passing to the right of the farm buildings, a stile can be located in front of the cottages to the right of a vehicular entrance to the farm buildings. Once onto the tarmac road in front of the cottages turn left along it and after 50 metres follow it around the right-hand bend to walk through the village of Tichborne.

A visit to St Andrew's church can be made by taking the first tarmac road on the left uphill for 100 metres. Follow the tarmac road around to the right in front of the Old School House (dating from 1843 and now a private residence) to reach the entrance to the church. Part of it dates from the mid 11th century and its interesting history is recounted in a guide book available inside. On leaving the entrance to the church turn immediately left to pick up a footpath running downhill between hedges onto a track near the tarmac road through the north-western end of the village. By turning right on reaching the track and then left north-eastward on reaching the road, you will find the Tichborne Arms on the right in 100 metres. This is a modern building; the original pub was burned down in 1939.

If you do not wish to visit the pub, turn left along the track to go north-north-east out of the village and then down into a shallow valley. Follow the track as it climbs up the other side, ignoring the footpath along a farm track to the right, and where the track turns left to go westward continue northward into the south-east corner of a field. Continue to climb in the same direction up the eastern boundary of the field and, just before the north-eastern corner of the field and immediately after passing the only tree on the hedge boundary, there is a stile at the point where the right-of-way crosses over into the field to the east. Once into that field turn left and continue up the western boundary in the same direction as before. On reaching the north-western corner turn left and back into the north-eastern corner of the field you were in two minutes earlier and continue westward along its northern boundary. Ignore the gap in the hedge leading into the field to the north and continue to the corner of the field where you enter the woodland ahead.

Once over a crude stile continue westward along a gulley or ditch which demarcates the route of the right-of-way out into the field to the west. On reaching the field follow a line of oak trees to the north-eastern corner, with fine views westward to Cheesefoot Head. Leave the field via a farm accessway onto the Alresford Road dual carriageway. Cross the road carefully and turn right to enter the layby where the walk started.

Historical Notes

Tichborne: There is a wealth of local history associated with the Parish of Tichborne and a good appreciation of the area can be obtained by reading the booklet *A History of Tichborne* by E Roberts and E Crockford. The scope of this booklet with its old photographs relates to the area covered by this walk.

Two local legends are worth recounting, the first concerning the field called 'The Crawls' mentioned above. In the 13th century the wife of Sir Richard Tichborne, Lady Mabella, was dying. She was desirous of leaving a charitable bequest to enable the distribution of a dole of bread to the poor who may choose to attend at Tichborne House on Lady Day to apply for it. Such a bequest would need to be related to some land if it was to last for any length of time. Her husband who seems to have been less than enthusiastic about the idea agreed to give the corn produced by the land that his wife could crawl around while a brand was alight. Lady Mabella, despite her condition, succeeded in crawling around the 23 acre field that bears the name The Crawls and this was the origin of the Tichborne Dole.

In the church of St Andrew there is a plaque memorial to Richard, the son of Sir Richard Tichborne who died at the age of 18 months in the 17th century at a time when the curse of a gypsy was greatly feared. Having declined a gypsy woman's request at Tichborne House for food a curse was placed on the young Richard with the threat that he would die by drowning on a specific day. In order to reduce the chances of the prediction coming true the servants were ordered to take the young lad onto the downs well away from the river Itchen. Alas when they were distracted from their duties on Gander Down the lad fell out of his carriage and drowned in a cart rut full of water.

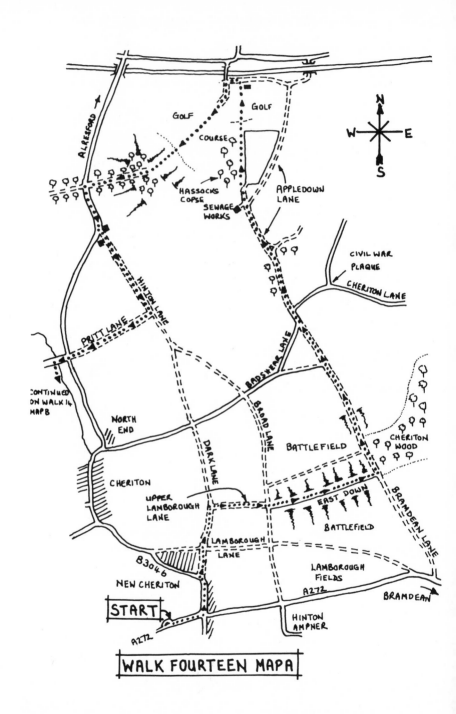

WALK FOURTEEN MAP A

The Cheriton Civil War Battlefield

Introduction: There are no pock-marked walls, deserted armaments or derelict defence positions to see, just tranquil leafy lanes, shallow downland valleys and hedgerows that saw fierce fighting on one eventful day over 200 years ago. From New Cheriton the walk runs along the ridge, the centre of the battle, to Cheriton Wood with good views. Then it is along more unsurfaced lanes up and down hill, through Hassocks Copse and across the golf course to New Alresford. The return route on this circular walk is via the downs above Tichborne Park and down to Cheriton Mill where the Itchen Way is joined following the river south to Cheriton and its church. From Cheriton the walk goes uphill to obtain good views of Hinton Ampner Park before descending back to New Cheriton. A classic Hampshire walk.

Distance: A walk of 6½ miles (10.5 km) with lots of ups and downs on mainly wide grassy lanes used a lot by agricultural vehicles in harvesting or ploughing periods. Boots are needed. This is a highly recommended walk.

Parking: There is an ideal layby on the north side of the A272 just west of its junction with the B3046 at New Cheriton.

Bus Services: The village of New Cheriton is on the Hampshire Bus Company's route 67 from Winchester via Alresford and West Meon to Petersfield. It is also served by Alder Valley bus company's service 241 from Kilmeston to Alresford.

Itchen Way – Tichborne to Cheriton: This eleventh stage of the walk starts at Cheriton Mill, two thirds of the way through Walk Fourteen (page 111) and continues to the bridge over the Itchen outside Cheriton Primary School in Cheriton. Then turn to the start of Walk Fifteen to continue the walk to the source of the river.

The Walk: From the junction of the A272 and the B3046 at New Cheriton go northwards along the latter. After 200 metres a tributary of the Itchen flows under the road and 50 metres beyond that the road bends to the left. At this point bear right uphill on a gravel track called Dark Lane. It turns to a path in a gulley and 200 metres from the road the crossroads with Lamborough Lane is reached. Go straight across and on uphill along Dark Lane, now a grassy track between hedges for 350 metres to another crossroads, with the footpath to Cheriton on the left along which this walk will return and Upper Lamborough Lane on the right. Take the latter to start a walk along a ridge towards Cheriton Woods visible to the east.

Upper Lamborough Lane is a grassy track between hedges and after 600 metres the crossroads with Broad Lane is reached in a slight dip in the ridge. Cross over to continue straight on up through a side gate and into a field to the east to follow the southern boundary eastward. There are good views north and west. After ½ mile at the south-east corner of the field, leave by a side gate out into the leafy Bramdean Lane on the western side of Cheriton Wood. Turn left here, but before doing so admire the view south towards Hinton Ampner. This ancient lane goes downhill just inside the boundary of the woods but with distinct banks on either side. A bridleway is passed going west, and then at the valley bottom the woods to the east end and the lane leads uphill between hedges. On attaining the crest of the ridge it is down the other side ignoring a substantial farm track off to the left, to continue in a northward direction up and over another slight hill before ascending to reach the tarmaced Badshear Lane. Follow the road northward for 70 metres until it turns right eastward and is then called Cheriton Lane.

There is a monument to the Cheriton battle ¼ mile east along Cheriton Lane, but this walk continues northward up Appledown Lane which is a chalk surfaced roadway in a slight gulley. In 200 metres the crest of a ridge is reached where there is a brick building on the right-hand side of the lane. Continue to follow this substantial lane as it begins to descend for 100 metres and then levels out and 100 metres later forks with a scrubby copse on the right. Take the left fork which is a substantial track, dropping downhill slightly and then up the other side, continuing generally in a northwards direction with trees and coppice either side of the lane. Descending into a shallow valley a junction of five tracks is reached at the entrance to Alresford Sewage Treatment Works where Apple-down Lane, the larger track, bears right. Look for a less obvious grassy vehicular track straight ahead which descends immediately into a slight dip. In 100 metres the vehicular track leads into a field. At this point pass to the left of the entrance where there is a pathway which continues northwards just inside Hassock's Copse running down its eastern boundary, descending all the way towards the roar of the traffic on the Alresford Bypass. The field on the east side of the copse ends and the first of the greens on the Alresford Golf Course appears.

Carry straight on northwards across the track signposted to the 14th tee. Now the golf course is on both sides of the path and as a brick and flint-faced building appears take care as a fairway has to be crossed to pass to the left of the building and through a side gate into a fenced bridleway above the Alres-ford Bypass. Turn left here towards a footbridge over the bypass but do not cross it. On reaching it turn left along the bridleway to Cheriton which starts as a track between wooden post and rail fencing. Where the fencing ends bear right slightly and continue south-westward across a fairway following the waymarks for the Wayfarers Walk which you have now joined. Continue on across three more fairways, following a line of posts topped with blue paint. With luck you will reach the other side of the golf course safely! A steep slope lies ahead. Follow a track along the right-hand side of a hedge, heading up

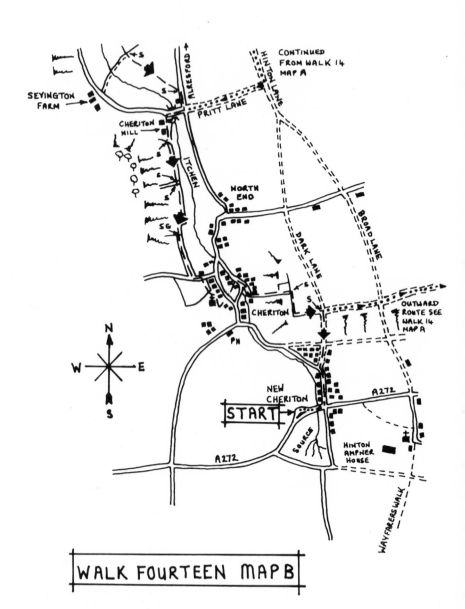

WALK FOURTEEN MAP B

in the direction of a wood on the skyline. The view improves dramatically to the north with a view over New Alresford and, beyond, the countryside covered in Walk Eleven of this book. Having admired the view continue straight on into the wood and over the top of the ridge and begin the descent along a wide grassy track between the remainder of an avenue of trees leading down towards Tichborne House.

On reaching the busy road between Alresford and Cheriton turn left south along the road for 200 metres and, immediately on the left after the first house, turn down a lane leading to a large modern barn. Passing to the left of the barn, continue along Hinton Lane, a grassy track initially up the east side of a field with views across towards Sevington Farm and Gander Down beyond. Three hundred metres from the barn the track returns to being a normal unsurfaced lane between thick hedges. It is a steady climb to the crest of the hill from which there are views towards Cheriton to the south. Just over the ridge turn right down Pritt Lane, a grassy track running downhill towards Cheriton Mill in the valley bottom.

On reaching the road between Alresford and Cheriton again, cross straight over along the minor road to Tichborne. **The Itchen Way** has now linked up with the Wayfarers Walk for the next section through to Cheriton. After crossing over the river Itchen, Cheriton Mill lies to the left-hand side of the road. The footpath to Cheriton leaves the road at the mill entrance, passing between the old mill and the farm buildings next to it and straight on through a field gate and up a grassy track passing to the east of the house. Respect the occupant's privacy and continue up the grassy track above the sluice channel feeding the old mill to a stile leading into the field to the south. Continue along the eastern and lower side of the field to the south-eastern corner, over a double stile at this point and along the eastern side of the next field. As you reach the south-eastern corner the hamlet of North End is across the other side of the Itchen. In the south-eastern corner cross over a stile next to a field gate to continue along the west side of the hedge, one field removed from the river. The footpath is now along a track fenced on both sides. After 200 metres a stile leads out onto a tarmaced road.

Turn left along the road and in 100 metres turn right through a kissing gate into the field to the south to go along the eastern boundary to another kissing gate leading into a graveyard. The footpath passes to the left or east side of the church ahead and out at the main pedestrian entrance in the south-eastern corner. If you take your boots off before entering, the church of St Michael dating from the 12th century is worth visiting (a contribution to its upkeep would be appreciated I am sure). Leave the churchyard by the main pedestrian entrance and after 50 metres you are out onto the main road through the village of Cheriton. Cross over the road and continue straight on along a narrow surfaced path across the village green and over a footbridge over a tributary of the river Itchen. Go straight on, passing to the left of the post office along a pathway out onto a minor road on the east side of the village.

Turn left and in 30 metres turn right across a minor road bridge over the river Itchen and right past the Cheriton Primary School. Here those following the through route on **The Itchen Way** leave this walk and continue from the start of Walk Fifteen.

To continue this walk follow this road south-eastward for 50 metres to where it ends at a point where there are two footpaths, one leading south called Back Alley and one on the left going eastward called Jane Long's path. Take the latter which is part of the Wayfarers Walk. It climbs steadily out of the village and is fenced on both sides until nearing the crest of a ridge when a field is entered. Continue straight along the southern boundary of the field to a stile on the south-eastern corner. A good view opens up to the east across the Cheriton Civil War battlefield. Once over the stile turn right and go to the south-western corner of the field where there is a view over New Cheriton and across the valley to the grounds of Hinton Ampner House. From the south-western corner go to the south-eastern corner along the southern boundary fence, ignoring a hunting gate leading into the field to the south. At the south-eastern corner cross over a stile and out onto grassy Dark Lane at the point mentioned earlier on the outward route. The return journey is now the reverse of that route.

Turn right and follow Dark Lane downhill towards New Cheriton. On reaching the first of an estate of bungalows continue across another vehicular track called Lamborough Lane. Go straight on down along the eastern boundary of the estate along a continuation of Dark Lane in a gulley to come out onto a more established vehicular track which leads to a tarmac road between Cheriton and New Cheriton.

Turn left and follow the road and in 300 metres the junction with the A272 is reached. Turn right and climb the hill to the layby where the walk began.

Historical Notes

The Battle of Cheriton: The Roundheads assembled on Monday 25th and Tuesday 26th March 1644 in the valleys around the villages of Warnford and East and West Meon. Also on Tuesday, after a council of war at Winchester, the Royalist forces led by Lord Hopton set out to surprise the enemy. On Wednesday the Roundheads had a general rendezvous at East Meon under the command of Sir William Waller. The Roundheads attempted to cut off the Royalists from their base at Winchester and the Royalists raced for the security offered by Alresford and the nearby downs where they spent the Wednesday night. The Roundheads camped in Lamborough Fields near Hinton Ampner, Sir William Waller staying with Lady Stukeley at Hinton House.

Thursday 28th March 1644 was spent by both sides locating the enemy and in minor skirmishes. At the end of the day the Royalists had advanced and lay along the ridge on the top of which runs the extension of Upper Lamborough Lane to Bramdean Lane used in this walk. The Roundheads were lower down along Cheriton Lane and south of what is now the A272. A tense night followed, each party within sight and sound of the other's position. At dawn Waller sent 1,000 musketeers into Cheriton Wood to the east of Bramdean Lane and the Royalist positions. The Royalists, however, outflanked them in the wood and drove them back. On the Royalist right flank, near Broad Lane below Hinton Ampner, the Royalists had engaged the Roundheads at the bottom of the hill, setting fire to the village of Hinton Ampner, but the wind turned the smoke and the Roundhead horse successfully countercharged. By noon the opposing forces were engaged all along the line. In early afternoon 2,000 Royalist cavalry went down onto the Roundheads along Bramdean Lane into a common but with heavy losses were forced to retreat back up the hill. For over three hours there was a fierce cavalry battle. By three or four in the afternoon the Roundhead musketeers on the east and west wings were pushing back their adversaries from hedgerow to hedgerow. The Royalists were allowed time to retreat as the Roundheads did not press home the advantage. The Royalist forces turned and withdrew to Alresford which they left burning and went onto Basing House by one o'clock in the morning. After a day's rest they retreated to Reading.

Cheriton to the Source of the Itchen

Introduction: If I had to choose a short circular walk on a clear day for a visitor to the County of Hampshire which showed the countryside at its best this would be it. The attractive village of Cheriton with its 12th century church of St Michael has a wide variety of pleasant architecture. The river Itchen, a dappled brook of many channels at the beginning of its journey, has interesting springs at the source south of New Cheriton. Wide views of rolling downland, green lanes, the magnificent splendour of Hinton Ampner House and its ornamental gardens and the church of All Saints make this route a pleasure to behold. Cheriton also has the Flower Pots Inn, a quaint, unspoilt place of refreshment before or after the walk. What more could you ask?

Distance: A walk of less than 3½ miles (5.3 km). Only if there has been wet weather or there is wet grass is there a need for boots but stout footwear is required. A walk suitable for all the family.

Parking: There is ample room in Cheriton for casual parking but not one car park, so park sensibly in the village, do not cause an obstruction, and there is no need to park near the start because there is much to see in the village itself.

Bus Services: The village of Cheriton is on the Hampshire Bus Company's route No 67 from Winchester via Alresford and West Meon to Petersfield; and also on the route of Alder Valley bus company's service 241 from Kilmeston to Alresford.

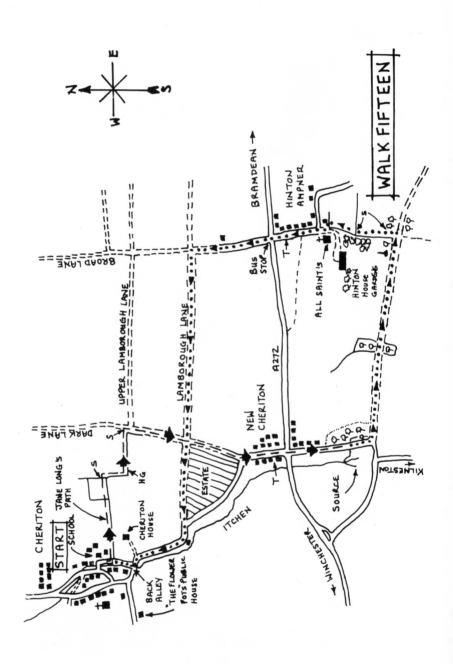

WALK FIFTEEN

Itchen Way – Cheriton to the Source: This final twelfth stage starts with Walk Fifteen at the Cheriton Primary School and follows the route of the walk until the source, south of New Cheriton, is reached where this long distance path ends. There is a bus service back to Winchester along the A272.

The Walk: The starting point for this walk is the bridge over the river Itchen outside the Cheriton Primary School at the eastern side of the village. The school is on a short length of road which should be followed south-eastward for 50 metres to where it ends at a point where there are two footpaths, one leading south called Back Alley and one on the left going eastward called Jane Long's path. Take the latter, named after the Long family who occupied Cheriton House to the south of the path from 1872 to 1875. It is part of the Wayfarers Walk and it climbs steadily out of the village and is fenced on both sides until you near the crest of a ridge when a field is entered. Continue straight on along the southern boundary of the field to a stile in the south-eastern corner. A good view opens up to the east across the Cheriton Civil War battlefield. (See Walk Fourteen) Once over the stile turn right and go to the south-western corner of the field where there is a view over New Cheriton and across the valley to the grounds of Hinton Ampner House. From the south-western corner continue to the south-eastern corner along the southern boundary fence ignoring a hunting gate leading into the field to the south. At the south-eastern corner cross over a stile and out into grassy Dark Lane. Turn right (the Wayfarers Walk is signposted straight on) and follow the grassy lane downhill towards New Cheriton. On reaching the first of an estate of bungalows, continue across another vehicular track called Lamborough Lane and straight on down along the eastern boundary of the estate along a continuation of Dark Lane in a gulley to come out onto a more established vehicular track which leads to a tarmac road between Cheriton and New Cheriton.

The river Itchen is to the west of the road. Turn left and follow the road and in 300 metres, after a telephone box, the junction with the A272 is reached with a petrol filling station on the other side. Cross over and continue south along the Kilmeston Road through the remainder of New Cheriton. The source of the river Itchen, which is the minor stream in the fields to the right, is reached after you have passed the last bungalow. Ahead to the right of the road is a private field with some large springs with water channels leading from them, and to the left of the road in a belt of trees is one very large one. Although they can be dry in summer, winter transforms the area as the water table rises. This is the end of the Itchen Way, the exploration of this famous Hampshire river is complete.

Continuing this circular walk follow the road to a point near the south-eastern corner of the field where there is a sharp right-hand bend and to the left there is a right-of-way heading eastwards along the southern boundary of the park and grounds of Hinton Ampner House. Going eastward there is first the shelter belt adjacent to the road and then an open field to the north with views across the valley to the south. The right-of-way is fenced on both sides and after ¼ mile it goes through another tree shelter belt and continues east between fences with fields to the south and to the north Hinton Park, the grounds in front of the House, which is now visible. After passing an ornamental stone pillar on the left and just before another group of trees the point is reached where the Wayfarers Walk crosses this right-of-way.

Turn left to follow the footpath to Tichborne and Alresford which goes through a kissing gate and out into the south-eastern corner of the field to the north. Follow the western boundary of this field uphill to cross over a stile in the north-western corner. Then continue up the western boundary of the next field, this time with the gardens of the house on the left. Do not cross a private stile or enter gates into the gardens but continue right up the western side of the field to the north-western corner where there is a kissing gate next to a field gate leading into a tarmac road opposite All Saints' church, Hinton Ampner. To the left of it the house can be glimpsed. Turn right along the road out of the grounds of the house through the ornamental gates. Continue on down Hinton Hill, joining another road coming from the east with an array of picturesque houses and cottages on the right. The road leads down to the A272. Just before the junction there is a telephone box on the left. On reaching the main road, cross straight over into Broad Lane. (Note there is a bus stop on the west side of the junction.)

Broad Lane crosses a shallow valley where in wet weather there are more springs adding to the flow in the Itchen. Follow the lane past Primrose Cottages on the right where the tarmac roadway reduces to a flint surfaced track and on uphill for 200 metres when a crossroads of minor lanes is reached. The Wayfarers Walk is signposted straight on, but turn left here westward along the wide level grassy Lamborough Lane, heading towards Cheriton. The site of a long barrow is in the field to the north. After ⅓ mile another crossroads of minor lanes is reached, one which you will have encountered earlier in the walk. Continue straight on along the north side of a housing estate along Lower Lamborough Lane as it gently descends to meet the road between Cheriton and New Cheriton.

Turn right to follow the road with the Itchen just on the western side. The road bends around to the right and then there is a short straight section with the Itchen running along the side of the road. At the next left-hand bend the river Itchen goes under the road. Here take a path on the right called Back Alley, close to the entrance of Cheriton House which follows the eastern bank of the river to come out onto the minor road where the walk started. If you are lucky you might see the blue flash of a kingfisher.

Historical Notes

All Saints' Church, Hinton Ampner: A very old church this, which still contains Saxon ornamentation and an internal doorway. It was largely rebuilt in the 13th century although the proportions and plan of the earlier church were preserved. There are marble monuments to the former occupiers of the adjoining Hinton House and several 17th century brasses. The timber bell turret contains three bells, two from 1603 and one dated 1619. In 1970 a subterranean vault was discovered at the foot of the altar steps. Mounted on the south wall of the nave are two large monuments brought from St Mary's church, Laverstoke on its demolition in 1952.

Hinton House, Hinton Ampner: The home of the successive families of Stewkeley, Stawell, Legge and Dutton, this has been rebuilt five times in 400 years, the last time after being gutted by fire in 1960. The last most respected occupier, Ralph Dutton, lavished a lifetime of care and restoration on it before it passed to the National Trust. The gardens are a mixture of formal layout and informal planting with every corner offering something new to look at. The book *A Hampshire Manor*, written by Ralph Dutton and published in 1968 by B T Batsford Ltd recounts the history of the house. Open from near the end of March to the end of September the house and gardens are well worth a visit as part of this walk. For the current opening hours see National Trust literature or contact their Southern Region Office at Polesden Lacey, Dorking, Surrey. (0372) 53401.

APPENDIX

Itchen Valley Country Park

Eastleigh Borough Council have acquired 178 hectares (440 acres) of land to the east of the airport and the Itchen Navigation. This irregular tract of land stretches from near Mans Bridge up to a point just south of the Eastleigh to Portsmouth railway line. It is a varied site which includes a 101 hectare (250 acre) nature reserve located between the Navigation and the river Itchen made up of disused water meadows with, to the east, woodland, grazing land and a 16 hectare (40 acre) field for informal recreation incorporating High Hill, at 27 metres the highest point at this side of the valley.

The Park is reached via an unsurfaced gravel roadway from Allington Lane (just north of where it crosses the M27) between the B3037 at Fair Oak and the A27 at West End. Two hundred metres from Allington Lane, after descending into a shallow valley, a cattle grid is crossed and the roadway then ascends with pine woodland to the east until a new reception centre for visitors is reached. The road bends to the right slightly and enters a pine forest where there is a group of five car parks. Two waymarked trails/walks have been laid out by the Borough Council which are illustrated on the following maps and there is also a separate trail for horse riders which passes just to the east of the car parks.

The Forest Trail: The heart of the higher eastern part of the Park is a large field surrounded by woodland at the eastern end of which is High Hill. The entrance road which provides access to the car parks continues north for 100 metres to this field. Turn left on entering the field and double back into the woods to follow a route, keeping just inside the pine forest to follow a route around the south, west and part of the north side of the field before returning diagonally back across the field to the start. One kilometre in length, this short walk can be extended by visiting High Hill where there are some picnic tables.

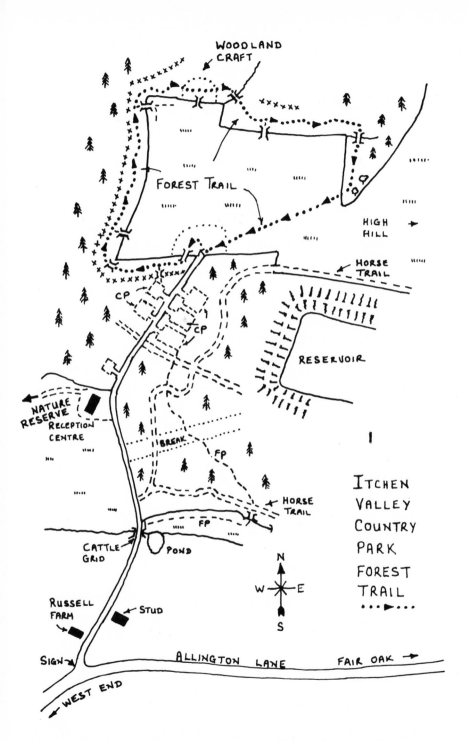

Woods and Meadows Walk: This one kilometre walk leaves the south-eastern corner of the car parks on the eastern side of the entrance road. The footpath enters High Woods crossing the horse riders route, then across a break in the wood and then across the horse riders route before entering the hay meadow called Moorlands Mead. Follow the waymarks west to the end of the field, past the pond and across the entrance road. The path continues along the south side of the grazing field opposite the edge of the flat meadows of the river Itchen before turning north to return to the car parks via a picnic site and the visitors centre.

For more information on the park and the activities arranged for visitors contact the Department of Leisure and Tourism, Eastleigh Borough Council, Civic Centre, Leigh Road, Eastleigh, SO5 4YN.

WOODS AND MEADOWS WALK ••••▶••••

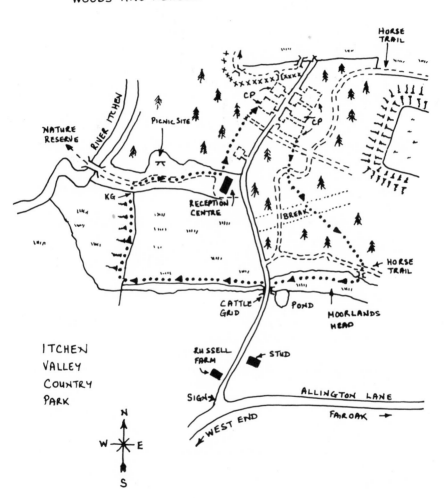

HORSE TRAIL

RIVER ITCHEN

NATURE RESERVE

PICNIC SITE

CP

CP

KG

RECEPTION CENTRE

BREAK

HORSE TRAIL

CATTLE GRID

POND

MOORLANDS MEAD

ITCHEN VALLEY COUNTRY PARK

RUSSELL FARM

STUD

SIGN

ALLINGTON LANE

WEST END

FAIROAK →

N
W ○ E
S

Further Reading

Hampshire and the Isle of Wight, Arthur Mee (Hodder and Stoughton)

The Solent Way, Barry Shurlock (Hampshire County Council Recreation Department)

The Southampton Guidebook, (Milestone Publications 1987)

The River Itchen, Noreen O'Dell (Paul Cave Publications)

Hamwic: Southampton's Saxon Town, Sharon Pay (Milestone Publications 1987)

Southampton Hall of Aviation, (Official Brochure)

The Story of Jesus Chapel commonly called Pear Tree Church, D E Corps (1985)

Excavations at Clausentum, Southampton 1951–54, M Aylwin Cotton and P W Gathercole (HMSO 1958)

The Southampton and Netley Railway, Edwin Course (City of Southampton 1973)

The Southampton Natural History Guide, Southampton Schools Conservation Corps (1987)

Guide to St Mary's, South Stoneham, (at the church)

The Itchen Navigation, Edwin Course (Southampton University Industrial Archaeology Group 1983)

Estllie from 1086 – 1936, (Eastleigh Borough Council and Hampshire County Museum Service)

A Protest Meeting at Bishopstoke, (The Eastleigh and District Local History Society Occasional Paper No 15)

Memories of Old Eastleigh and Bishopstoke, Maureen Westwood (1985)

Peter New's Rambling Round Eastleigh and District, revised by Gordon Cox (1984)

George, Prince of Wales and Mrs Maria Fitzherbert, (Eastleigh and District Local History Society Special Paper No 8)

Brambridge, Katharine M R Kenyon

A Portrait of Otterbourne

Compton and Shawford, Austin Whitaker (Published by Barbara Large and Austin Whitaker, Compton 1985)

The History of The Hospital of St. Cross, Paul Cave (Paul Cave Publications Ltd)

Guide to St. Mary the Virgin, Twyford, (at the church)

Saint Catharine's Hill, Winchester, C F C Hawkes, J N L Myres and C G Stevens (Warren and Son 1930)

The Winchester Story, Barry Shurlock (Milestone Publications 1986)

Guide to the Winnall Moors Nature Reserve, (Hampshire and Isle of Wight Naturalists' Trust Ltd)

Worthy History, No. 2, (Kings Worthy Local History Group 1987)

Guide to St. Mary's Church, King's Worthy, (King's Worthy Local History Group 1987)

Easton and its Church, (at the church)

Guide to The Church of St. John the Baptist, Itchen Abbas, I Sanderson (at the church, 1980)

Guide to Avington Park, (at the house, 4th Edition)

Guide to St. Mary, Itchen Stoke, I Sanderson (The Redundant Churches Fund)

Guide to St. Peter's Church, Ovington, (at the church)

The Alresford Trail, (Compiled and produced on behalf of the Friends fo St. John the Baptist, Alresford 1982)

A walk around New Alresford, Laurence Oxley (1987)

A History of Tichborne, E Roberts and E Crockford

Cheriton, E Crockford

Cheriton 1644 – The Campaign and the Battle, John Adair (Roundwood Press 1973)

Guide to All Saint's Church, Hinton Ampner, (at the church)

A Hampshire Manor, Ralph Dutton (Batsford 1968)

Sketches of Hampshire, John Duthy (1839, Reprinted by Laurence Oxley 1972)

The Wayfarers Walk, (Hampshire County Council Recreation Department)

British Regional Geology – Hampshire Basin and Adjoining Areas, (HMSO)

Public Transport
BRITISH RAIL Network South East, Waterloo Station, London SE1 8SE – Passenger train information service on Southampton (0703) 229393 or Winchester (0962) 56453
MID-HANTS RAILWAY PLC, Alresford Station, Alresford, SO24 9JG. Tel: Winchester (0962) 734200
ALDER VALLEY, Halimote Road, Aldershot, Hampshire GU11 3EG. Tel: Aldershot (0252) 23322 or Alton (0420) 83787
CLASSIC BUSES LTD, 2 Wales Street, Winchester
HAMPSHIRE BUS COMPANY LIMITED, Eastleigh House, Upper Market Street, Eastleigh SO5 5QY. Tel: Winchester (0962) 52339 or Basingstoke (0256) 464501
MERVYN'S COACHES, 3 Chapel Close, Dummer, Basingstoke, Hampshire RG25 2AB. Tel: Dummer (025675) 719
OAKLEY COACHES, Beach Arms Service Station, Andover Road, Oakley, Basingstoke RG23 7HB. Tel: Basingstoke (0256) 780731
SOUTHAMPTON CITYBUS, 226 Portswood Road, Southampton SO9 4XS. Tel: (0703) 553011/701163

The Ramblers' Association
For details of membership, information on walking as a hobby and the address of your nearest Group write to 1/5 Wandsworth Road, London SW8 2XX or telephone 01 582 6878.